# COMBING BACK THROUGH TIME: PAUL STAPLETON'S STORY

## BY
## MICHAEL ATKINSON
## M.Sc.

Combing Back Through Time:
Paul Stapleton's Story

By
**Michael Atkinson**
**M.Sc.**

First published in Great Britain by
Aultbea Publishing Limited in 2006

First Edition

Copyright © 2006 Michael John Atkinson

ISBN 1 905517 08 4

Printed by Thomson Litho

Cover design by Al Knight

**Aultbea Publishing**
28 Church Street
Inverness
IV1 1HB
www.aultbeapublishing.com

# COMBING BACK THROUGH TIME: PAUL STAPLETON'S STORY

To my wife, Diane, whose strengths I admire, including her patience – which I have tried.
*Michael Atkinson*

# CHAPTER ZERO:
## PAST ANXIETIES, FORETHOUGHTS AND MINDSET

I am Paul - just plainly that, a name which cannot be shortened or for which there is no nickname. For that I am thankful, though here I am already in one of my obsessions, when I find an empty headed moment – names and their significance. I was hoping that my next move to university would stretch my imagination at least a bit over this idling thought mind-gap, which gives space to what my better self sees as silly childhood anxieties, such as still wanting to express my view of this in full:

I was named in short after my father, Jean-Paul, and straight away, I do remember thinking when I was young, that with half my dad's name I was maybe set up to be half as successful. So you can see that my attitude of mind was made at an early stage, to expect relative inadequacy. Though Paul was actually my mother's choice in a sort of commemorative link to her early romance with my father, who had the name she fell in love with, the way she does with most French things. Just as when she pronounces it with emphasis on the 'L', more of an 'elle' sound, often said in phrase, "Oui Jean-Paul," to which my father would complete in their tiresome double act, "Ah Tish, you spoke French." Thinking of Gomez Addams, from their TV era, using the shortened version of my mother's name Katicia, her parents being Gilbert and Sullivan fans. But here her parents must have liked purely the name, without regard to the character, as I now understand that it was the name given to a figure of fun and pity in the opera. Anyway it was her special regard for my father that led to me being simply Paul, coupled with my father's general dislike of hyphenated names. I sometimes wonder why not Jean, but then in

English naming this is female. Mind you I could have fancied Gene, though short for Eugene, it has the same English pronunciation. Oh well, anyway such references are the privileged choice of our parents and at least mine is simple, straightforward to spell and not mistakable. So that's me, Paul Stapleton, and taking the view further, even the surname sounds to be of a plain origin as it speaks of 'staple diet' or 'plain town' person, or for that matter will I ever get out of here being 'stapled' to the 'town'. But in spite of what associations I can make of it, it would seem to others as someone most unlikely to be remembered well. Unlike a memorable name such as Tab Hunter or the more rugged sounding Rip Torn of Hollywood fame, or a name with a ring to it as Ringo Starr has – literally.

Whatever we may be named, prospectively famous or not, generally speaking, it holds true to say that people born within the last half century have had good opportunities to better themselves and in general are expected to achieve more than their parents. One thing though that makes it very difficult is when parents are established high achievers. They certainly want their kids to make their own way in the world, but often can't share any of their important daily activities, from a career perspective with their kids, as it isn't an easy fit into everyday family life. For they exist too far apart.

There was a young man called George Dyson, whose father Freeman Dyson was a well noted Physicist from the fifties/sixties, and he escaped to a tree-house he had built ninety odd feet in the air over the Canadian west coast. He was essentially trying to escape the shadow of his father, whilst trying to establish some worth for himself with the highest tree-house on record. I empathise with that. My father is a Professor of History, a subject which in my early teens left me quite cold. After all, I could not understand why any good level headed fellow would want to read books on Hitler for enjoyment.

Admittedly, there maybe some difference in my case, as he didn't really overshadow my interests. I was much more stimulated by my chosen direction of science and technology. Wanting to read books with a mainly technical content, using them rather than reading front to back.

Then for weekend recreation, something else that put me at odds with the average teenager, I preferred to look at planets moving around a star field than say players on a playing field. Far from 'normal' in this respect maybe, but then I never understood why we pay such a lot to have men chase a ball just as dogs do, the difference just being a set of rules and team play. It puzzles me how we can applaud people using their sub-conscious minds in this way, which is what repetitive/reliable action stems from, like the set piece free-kick, or the tennis service. The reader may understandably think that this view is of someone who was poor at it, and by and large that is true. Lack of developed skill was due in no small way to lack of interest, for at school I was amongst the leftovers, always playing with the less than eleven per side, once the stars had picked their teams. We used the unmarked ground beside the pitch, and had cricket stumps as makeshift goal posts. Having said all that, there wasn't much of a family tradition either, my father in particular viewed the pursuit of most games as a waste of time, and devotion to any game as a waste of a life. I don't think it was so much being steered away from such sporting games by my family, it was more my own desire to pull out of a kick around the neighbourhood square at our housing block, or the schoolyard. The school, being on the main road west offered the alternative playtime attraction of vehicle spotting, though I do acknowledge that that is more of an anorak's pastime or hobby. However, having a regular dose of atmospheric lead, from taking up the position next to the boundary fence, and with its believed affect on brain development, I had stored this experience in mind as a potential stock excuse for lack of achievement in later life. Such was my anxiety over expectation.

More reasonably, as I don't want to sound dismissive of those who are keen on sport, I do think that there is a place for recreation and it does have health benefits, but that's not to represent such popular sport as a way of life. Quite literally football, as the prime example, has become almost a modern 21st Century religion, and it produces millionaires too – such is the hold it has on our society. Though it is a fact that, over the last century or so, societies' rewards have shifted around. From sports pursuits starting amongst the lowest with often an honour and privilege basis only, to politics being a part-time activity and usually the preserve of city lawyers and businessmen with available time, to then scientists and technologists who have fallen down relative to their place in the Industrial Revolution which made the modern world. In turn, early Physical and Life as well as Social Scientists were often clergymen, who were amongst the most educated people with free (study) time in the first place, that is before science was seen as a worthy endeavour and a justified profession.

Maybe it's just a phase with me, but I can't help rating activities or skills by how much use they are when we get into difficulties. That is how much use to us on something like a desert island shipwreck. All sorts of things carry an accepted cost in a sophisticated economy, but it is very different in a disaster. Those that can produce shelter, drinking water and food. Those that have the rudiments of first-aid and nature cures, would all be better afforded - not forgetting boat builders. I suppose what I am trying to say is that I would prefer it if we were to acknowledge more those core activities and I prefer to see the recognition of real achievers, in something really representative of human development and the furthering of our cause. Whereas we do seem to attach more significance to lighter things, as if they're at the pinnacle of our achievement by this 21st Century. I mean, is it really what we have evolved to do, is it to become our main purpose? Did England achieve its second half of the 20th Century main purpose by winning the World Cup in 1966? We could be lead to think so. In seeking to rest my case, as I am writing this account largely retrospectively, I do now know by the summer of 2005 that a Scottish banknote is to bear the image of an American golfer – what does this say to real local achievers?

When it is said that the universe has developed to such an extent, that it is trying to understand itself through us, you can perhaps then see to my mind why all media stars from sport, pop, film and even politics are much the same, and not in the same league as were the likes of Faraday or Newton, to plug a couple of significance from the U.K. To have in the very least a unit of Universal measurement named after you for time ever after, really is more of a 'place in history' than being remembered for a crucial corner – either a football kick or a political speech to get out of one. As it was, Michael Faraday and his early mentor Humphrey Davies were among top crowd, drawing public performing orators of their day anyway. They were as eloquent as any of their contemporaries such as men of the law, and on top of that were great showmen. Let alone being uniquely responsible for their own discoveries and forward steps in our understanding. For that matter Laws such as Newton's as well as Boyles' and Hookes' remain as they were first stated, being seen more as original truths in their written doctrinal form.

Apart from being our first woman Prime Minister, Margaret Thatcher entered this office having the rare background of good science, and therefore higher level numeracy as well as exposure to technology. Being a working graduate Chemist, prior to an LLB as additional support to a political career. Why is it then that we continue to choose those who are trained in argument, legal procedures, and in some cases etiquette, but very little else as our leaders? Those who don't know a magnate from a magnet, who thought, until disputes got up to a fever pitch in 1999 demanding a government view, that G.M. food is something featured on GMTV. I won't start on nuclear power. For they don't even understand the mechanisms behind the water supply enough to see the logic in suggesting not to build houses in the South East – especially when today's communication technology removes the need for condensation of economic activity. We do need to see that this cannot be helped by people who think little more than water just comes out of a tap, let alone that electricity just comes from holes in the wall, and all as we live with incorrect assertions like 'product' literature describing building society 'services'. In essence we should not put people in charge of a technological society, who have a knowledge base that would not be out of place 200 years ago, and who show their true lack of understanding when they use what they see as fashionable technical terms incorrectly and out of place. A classic error, used more or less since the Space Age, is saying 'light years' to emphasise a long time, when in fact it is a measure of distance. Furthermore, those who do understand such fundamentals would not express themselves as being one hundred and ten percent certain, a value beyond the maximum hundred percent or a probability of one which equals certainty; also being one hundred and twenty percent confident has similar illogic. In the increasing habit of throwing speeches at problems, this lack of rigour also shows with the fashion for saying 'year-on-year', where this doesn't always mean the cumulative, for everything will increase year on year as would be displayed by an ogive, or cumulative frequency curve, unless one year has a negative score. Then they say 'going forward', where what is being referred to would be measured in time-series statistically and only goes forward, maybe up and down (for better or worse) but 'forward' all the same. Our conceptual thinking is challenged by 'a raft of robust measures going forward', if we need to imagine direction with a bow or stern, and it's a priority surely for the raft to be robust?

Anyway, whilst what I've written so far is just to let you know straight out my concerns, what 'makes me tick' or as they now say, 'where I am coming from', I was always told, by those close enough to me to be concerned, that thinking too much about the way of the world as a teenager can only lead to a dissatisfied life. That I should simply enjoy things more and face the better challenges that I can reach. When I reflect on that, I suppose I could save some of my deepest thoughts, and save all of my philosophy on life for my late years, after I've made my own journey through it.

# CHAPTER ONE:
## MY NEW FOUND FRIEND

So it is at this point that I start my story, which is about time. I do also mean that it is about time I started, though not with 'Once upon a time', as that would be too ordinary a start to this extraordinary tale. I believe it best to mention the first time I met the main man, not the hero, for I know that he would be unhappy about that, being the very modest guy I've come to know.

To set the scene:
We were outside on the loungers by the interview room at the University, both waiting for a confirmation interview to embark on their Applied Physics course. I glanced at this fellow next to me, who looked a bit older than me at eighteen, but not quite old enough to be a mature student, i.e. certainly under twenty-five. He was of a sturdy build, with a fresh healthy complexion and sun-bleached hair. He was to my mind someone likely to be used to more physical outdoor activity than me. Then I asked him, "Have you come far?" "Just along the road", came the reply. Then I just had time to say, "I live here too," when through the doorway came the words, "Mister Taylor please! Do come in and close the door." Then shortly after what was quite a brief interview, the door opened, and I heard the interviewee's voice carry with the acknowledgment, "Thank you Mister Rudden." With that I shuddered, knowing it was Doctor Rudden, as on the appointment letter. But then maybe I was preconditioned with the academic protocols more than most having a family member in the 'trade'. My father was a Professor at this very University. The lad came out alone, with what I hoped for him was nothing spoiling for that, then looked over to me and said, "They've asked

me to send you in next." I got up, and when walking past him he said, "It's Lewis by the way." I nodded with a smile replying, "I'm Paul, and I might see you on the course then." He smiled and with that we both turned attention to our respective next moves and parted company.

Some days later 'in the grand order of things', Lewis from my interview day became my new found friend in my equally new University college course. Well placed to get on, we laughed at the same quirks of the lecturers we were due to receive the great wisdom of. All this after the introductory week, in which we were treated to the colleges' definition of an informal and friendly start, to build up good spirits and level all of our new relationships.

Doing Applied Physics together meant that we were able to partner up for 'Labs.' and as is true of a lot of practical work, you were pretty much left to get on with it. Working against a programme controlled by the tutor, but only involving the tutor when you got acceptably stuck. I say this because their way was to stop everyone and ask if they needed the same coverage to save repeating themselves. Meaning that if you got unacceptably stuck, then you felt a fool with regard to the rapidly establishing class standard.

Lewis was older than most of us for a first year undergraduate, and this is because he had served a full apprenticeship at B.T. before joining the course, leaving school at 16 and coming in with BTEC qualifications in lieu of A levels. This meant he was a bit more laid back than most, having a 'trade' and some experience of the work-a-day world. Last time the rest of us looked around a room we were in school uniforms.

As the weeks progressed I sometimes wondered if Lewis was my best choice as a lab-partner for success, as he often seamed to skim the surface of the experimental work and this was as if it was unimportant to him. This together with his preoccupied attitude in the theory sessions led me to ask him about his interests and ambitions. He did confirm that he'd always wanted this course for study, but was beginning to think that he was only going to be interested in certain aspects of the curriculum, even though he seemed to accept that this was not a winning approach.

Lewis seemed quite a deep and somewhat mysterious fellow, even though he had answered readily when asked about his background. We had not met before, although we were both local to the college, my position being that my father lectured there. Lewis however, was a farmer's son, though not a good traditional farm-boy by his reckoning; but by all accounts he was the farming community's resident expert at repair and maintenance of all machinery, especially the instrumentation, which was getting used increasingly within mobile systems. He also kept up to date with the market gardening demands for timer and control systems for watering, ventilation and artificial sunlight pattern control, as well as the increasing interest in site security generally. Presumably then this was linked to his telecommunication background and interest. A talent as I discovered which took him far and wide at one time, before the modular replacement concept got a good foothold in the industry. This then brought more bench-work back to his home base – either way, giving him quite a busy time at weekends and evenings from much earlier on in his life as a school boy, and on through his apprentice days as a nice part-time earner. So no the wonder that, in spite of it being close to the farm, I hadn't seen him wasting it down at the village boozer's backroom, playing the slot pool tables and spending on the old jukebox, which my contemporaries and I did - when we had pocket money that is. Funny to talk of boozing pocket money, but by then we were eighteen-ish, or at least we felt legit at eighteen on average during our last sixth form year.

Getting more friendly with Lewis, I was on his invite up to their farm one day, when I asked him why he didn't go to the Agricultural County College ('Aggro-hall' as it was called) to study Agric. Engineering – seemed a natural thing to me. He acknowledged the point by saying, "Harper-Adams would have been the choice, they do a four year sandwich with good options on Mechanical Engineering and Farm Automation." I asked him what inspired him. To which he replied very specifically, "In the May and June of 1998, just at the time I would be firming up what to do career-wise at sixteen, I became aware that the Hughes Company's HGS-1 satellite had had difficulty getting a good geosynchronous orbit. They came up with the solution to send it round the moon, re-introducing it to a truer orbit on its return, which made it the first commercial comms. satellite to orbit the moon. It was a lesser article in the press, but it had me thinking straight away that people who can do this are truly capable, they are the real achievers with this work, and I want a piece of it. Hence my enrolment in a B.T. apprenticeship, leaving a farm 'management' career option behind." "What you say, Lewis, pleases me," I said, realising that he seemed to think just as I did, "I am with you all the way, in fact I'm very much of like mind." "Well, I am definitely a Science and Technology devotee – I'll show you something," he replied as he lead me into a remote barn, "and this is why!"

# CHAPTER TWO:
## THE REVELATION

Lewis pulled back an inner roller door, featured some way from the main old wooden hinged door, and past some rather historic, perhaps classic farm implements in various states of assembly. In this back section of this smaller of three barns, Lewis had the area well cleaned out and newly painted with a recent concrete floor. He also had a bench full of instrumentation but looking old and evidently army surplus. Then to be seen more clearly when he put the light on, within a marked out floorspace, was a shinny metal orb. I say 'orb', but then more correctly in place of the usual cross standing up on top there was a sort of spike.

"Looks like a large football," I said in the simplest terms to make light of the situation. "Your right enough," said Lewis, "large – in that it is an exact metre across, and yes those plates are the geometry of a modern football with twenty hexagons and twelve pentagons, but all for good reason my friend!" In accordance with what Lewis was saying was that very image, of a large shiny football, and as I studied it further I could see that it had one of the shaped plates open and hinged to the ground showing a camera lens. It also had wiring coming out of this hatch leading off onto the instrument bench. Talking up then, with a pace of excitement, I went on to explain my understanding of such geodesic shapes and the work of Buckminster Fuller. Including the fact that a more recent acknowledgment was to liken by name a sixty atom crystal shape of carbon, formed in zero gravity, as Buckminster Fullerine, or 'Bucky balls' to Curl, Kroto and Smalley, who got 1996's Nobel Prize for Chemistry. My statement was also my attempt at keeping on side and sounding useful. Lewis was listening but also made himself busy.

Then I asked outright, "Okay then, what's it for Lewis?" "It's a time machine," he said succinctly and very matter of fact. Before I could recompose my dropped jaw, he stopped what he thought was my emerging smile of ridicule by saying, "I am only showing and telling because I am bursting to share this with someone, and I trust you!" He was so straight faced about it that I found myself going with it and asked another lay question, "Where do you sit – it's a bit small isn't it?" I could feel my own disappointment at not asking questions worthy of a Physics student, but then I certainly didn't feel within my depth here, more especially when I considered what was Lewis' practical prior-hobby side of things. After all, my reputed reason for being on our course, was to stay away from my father's area of subject influence and because of deciding to go to the local college to keep the costs down, I had to be well out of the way of the Humanities Department. Seeing dad around the clock, at home and at the college would be setting me on a course for a joint honours degree in Madness with Frustration.

I knew Lewis did not answer straight back and I did not ask again, I just walked over to him at the bench. "There's maybe a few things I need to explain. You see, you can't travel or we can't travel, and besides there's nothing more we could do if we could go. You see, you can only go back in time and this," he said pointing, "will only observe, it can only see and it cannot hear. It therefore records visual images, and as there is no molecular interchange or influence with the scene, sound cannot be detected. Same goes of course for any interference with events or substance, there would certainly be no such thing as stepping out!" "So it's just a 'probe' then?" I said with another ill-considered choice of words, as if we all had one and there was some disappointment in this not being different or indeed better in some way. "Well actually," said Lewis, "it's really more of a time-comb than a probe, maybe a probe in purpose, but a comb in function, mode or method." Somehow, and gladly this time I did not just come out and say it, I did have the feeling that he wasn't just talking about combing through records of historical interest. Or like an Archaeologist or a Palaeontologist, combing through soil with a trowel looking for fragments of what once was.

Lewis went on to explain how the device probed through past time by combing space around itself. It had an ability for progression (or more correctly regression) in the fourth dimension (time) by moving 3D space around itself. Shifting by one metre at a time extremely quickly and by doing so, warped the space such that once it moved off the spot, it occupied an infinitely thin pointed cylinder of space (one metre tall). This is such that to an observer within the same time frame, it would be invisible and untouchable with it having the outside observer's occupied space warped around it. On the other hand, the view that the probe has is 360 degrees, such that a front mounted camera lens receives an image from all around it. Lewis then paused after this condensed explanation and looked up saying, "Don't be overly concerned if I've just thrown you with somewhat complex imagery, I am sure you'll get a better grip of it as we go further through it practically." As it happens, I was simply thinking that, in dangerous physical exploration, unmanned probes are becoming the norm. So this is the way of the modern world.

"How do you control it and receive the images then?" I asked, showing that I had taken in more than he had perhaps allowed for. "By recording, and with a bit of electronic processing, I can stretch them back to the original view totally around," Lewis replied. He continued to elaborate with, "It is done by showing it as consecutive images on a circular layout of monitor screens – over there!" He pointed at a still darkened corner of the barn, where I could see some low budget tellies circling an old Ekornes distinctively coloured (lagoon green as I later found out) swivel chair. They were also connected to the bench and, more specifically, a DVD player. "You must use a DVD recorder then?" I deduced. To which Lewis went on to explain why the latest contemporary high quality hard drive recorders don't work because of magnetism. The same thing would also have readily disqualified tapes, let alone other practical needs, whereas as he found laser products do return results. "In fact the DVD recorder has been 'the last page I've been waiting for in the book of success' you might say," he expressed. (I probably would not say it to him, but I thought, there is no way I could compete with this guy, he is a wordsmith as well!)

"Anyway, that's enough for today – fancy a coffee back at the house to refresh you before your walk over home?" Asked Lewis, as he turned down the lights and guided me back out. "Don't say much in front of the folks, in fact nothing about what you've seen. Even though it sounds unbelievable and would not be taken seriously by most, I still have a fear of careless talk." A comment Lewis rounded off with before we entered the house. So indeed we just sat with his mother for a while in front of the open fire as she knitted. His father, typical of a farmer with a dawn 'til dusk work plan, was in bed and so the household remained naturally quiet until I bade them goodnight and left.

When in turn I was able to get to bed, my mind was racing, thinking of the very idea of time travel, and so the following morning I was early into the college library. Thumbing through books all day there, I was beginning to feel a bit of a rebel having assignments to do, whilst putting every effort and time into something else. Not an approach to study my father would endorse, but still I could see it was more Lewis' style and certainly rewarding at that. After all, how should we define education, learning something of interest and use to you, or learning only what you are told or expected to.

In my reading, I was studying more of the philosophical aspects than the technical know-how, after all Lewis seems to have that. Though I do gather that he understands more how it works than why it works, and in a way that is not very different to the inventions throughout history.

From the first discovery of fire where there was no real understanding of what flame was, through to the introduction of the steam engine where a more recent study of Thermodynamics explains it. A great number of these have been developed empirically, rather than setting out with a theoretical model, and I do see that Lewis is no different.

I saw one view taken to be that there is no time, there is just progression, and that this is seen and experienced to go one way, with forward changes, in the very meaning of the word. That the difference between one time and another is a change of state, or that time is measured by the ticking clock of molecular movement, say crystalline oscillation of atoms, and at Absolute Zero (-273 degrees C or 0 degrees Kelvin) there is no molecular movement. There is no clock and therefore no time. Also in this association, from an idea originally expressed by Bose, is that at this temperature of zero energy molecules lose their structure and become one newly formed large atom. In fact a further reduction of energy state, or as Einstein viewed it, all their elementary particles merge into a single quantum state. It became labelled in 1924, as Bose-Einstein Condensate. A very still and time fixed world at this level.

Also outside of what we understand from Einstein, about relativity and time passing relative to the observer and therefore at different rates etc, it is made logically plain that going forward in time to what will be commonly shared future events is not possible and this is because they do not yet exist. Interestingly enough 'Relativity' as such is more correctly attributed to Galileo as far as the core understanding of relative velocity is concerned. It was the 'General' and 'Special' labels of Einstein's that took it further and into a necessarily new area of 'Thought Experiment' as he was really reaching 'out of this world' for the practicality of proof in the early 20th Century.

I also covered the time paradox of interference: The supposition that you discover that your great great grandfather (a man you did not know) as a young bachelor was responsible for some terrible episode of history, which we are still affected by today. Then you decide that it is best to go back and kill him. If you did then you would not exist and if so would not be able to.... and there are more similar to that. Another example is if you were able to talk to Leonardo Da Vinci about the fact that the 'Mona Lisa' would become so valuable, then you were able to convince him to do more of that style with a view to future riches. It would be the very fact that there were more that would affect its uniqueness and developed value, with this woman and the special mystery behind her mildly smiling expression. The consequence would be its developed value as a treasured possession, for it could well then be simply seen as part of a series exhibiting a style and nothing special.

Then there's a simple thought experiment, which says that as you look at your own reflection you are looking at an image which is slightly older than actual. So as a logical extension, if you placed a mirror half a light year away then the image would be one year old. This in itself is not very different to Einstein's reported first thoughts, when travelling from his local station, looking back at the station clock and considering moving away as fast as the image of the time came to him, therefore freezing time and so on.

Lewis indulged my keenness to talk some more about it when I caught up with him on Campus later that day, and with some discretion I picked a quiet corner of the Union Bar. "Yes," he said straight out, "I expect you do appreciate I need to be careful about knowledge of the work." He then mildly grunted out a laugh saying, "Mind around here they would just think we were talking some plot of a futuristic game or some other Science Fiction – they would not believe that it was practical Time-Travel." "Talking of 'practical'," I said, "I have clued myself up a bit better to understand it. So tell me more, how does it work?"

Lewis smiled, and said trustingly, "I'll tell you what I know or what I think I've found out, but you do realise that I am looking to some of our course to help me grasp the Theoretical Physics of it?" I nodded, and he continued, "I spent some time during my B.T. apprenticeship working on electrostatic problems, right up to lightning, and I became familiar with their kit. I then wondered how I could apply electrostatics to an agricultural setting and problems of dust around separators – threshing machines, combines and the like, very much a down to earth application. I made an earlier bench-top ball, much smaller, and it did need to approximate to a spherical shape to function. Not dissimilar to the globe shaped top from a Van der Graff's Generator out of a School Lab, which you may remember.

I experimented with the affects of different voltages - some pulsing. It was doing this that I notice a surface distortion, which I could tune in and out of with the voltage regulator. Really speaking it was sort of lens effect, it put me in mind of the sort of thing that Einstein wrote about (since proven) with the gravitational effects of massive Stella objects distorting the observed position and the apparent brightness of a star. The pentagonal and hexagonal plates or the 'football' look, apart from allowing me to make a globe from flat plates, are there to develop a sweeping or combing pattern with the electrostatic discharge." I humoured myself with the thought that for someone who's not a fan of football, here I was visualising a representation of one in awe. Lewis continued, "The plates are made of silver plated copper with insulation between them. The discharge path jumps these gaps, because of the coupled balanced and then imbalanced geometry of the shaped plates, having even then uneven numbers of corners for the charge to jump from, leading it to sweep across the surface. Whilst this would logically be randomised, because of the spin of the Earth the charge bolt pattern sweeps across the surface East West by this bias."

"A bit like the water round the plug hole phenomena because of the Coriolis Effect", I said, showing I was paying total attention, by referencing the way water tends to swirl in opposite directions as placed in the World's northern or southern hemispheres. Lewis confirmed this view, "Exactly! An otherwise random event with a small but effective influence, enough to tip the scales as it were." He could see I was all ears, so he went on, "So charge bolts with North South (top to bottom) polarity are running at about 'C', the velocity of light, and then they're sweeping round at the rotational speed of the earth at this latitude. Though this is something I am not dead sure of. Not just that value at our latitude, but whether or not there are other components of velocity in solar and galactic rotation, and for that matter galactic movement relative to a fixed point. Anyway, I don't have to get into that to solve anything, as I found that there is what I can only describe as an eddy around the sweeping charge and with the right voltage it appeared to have the force to, in a word, 'comb' the space back around itself."

"That must have been amazing," I said. "Certainly was," replied Lewis, "I worked on into the night, watching sectors disappear and reappear almost peeling it back and forward again with adjusted voltage tuning, working up to halfway and therefore calibrating a value for a total spatial jump. Next development was to pulse this voltage at its full value and add a presetable counter as well as scale up to the unit you've seen. The camera and recordable DVD are the essential additions for it to be at all useful." "Is the metre diameter to do with the calibration?" I asked. "Precisely that," Lewis added, "the counter will count the number of fully 'combed spatial-jumps' it is to make and we compute the number involved in a full revolution of this sector (this latitude) of the Earth equals one day, then compute the number of days I want it back to. Of course you might think logically that it would be quicker again nearer or as near as possible to the poles, being a shorter actual distance to a one day revolution. But then it must be relatively close to right angles in relation to the rotation, and this latitude itself has had to be limited by the magnetic control needed during travel, keeping it upright to maintain its own top and bottom in relation to the iron core. The optimum is 60 degrees, either North or South, and as it happens South is all ocean. That's not that North and land masses make things significantly slower, it's just easier for horizon referencing and less processing means less energy and less to go wrong – better benefits with longer journeys. The crust is 5 to 30 Km. thick, including ocean floors, as well as mountains and valleys, and it's about 9000 Km. to the iron core. It needs magnetic control, you see we cannot rely upon gravity alone well beyond something like 17 times the rotational speed of the earth - it would become detached - you could see that as a form of 'escape velocity'. Oh, and it's guided for the 23° axial tilt too."

"Where does it go? Er I mean…" Lewis interrupted my clumsy words, "I know what you're asking. It occupies a sort of 'non-space', dimensions of which as I mentioned before are one metre high and, infinitely, or more correctly totally thin. Put it this way, if it was here, we wouldn't see it, and not only that but we could walk 'through it' in a sense. Really we would be walking around it, within our own space, totally unhindered by it." "Okay, and you can only look back in time with it then?" I said. "Yes, and its 'look but don't touch'!" he quipped. "That certainly figures in with what is known or should I say believed from reading up a bit this morning," I confirmed. Being also somewhat assured by Lewis' expressed expectation that these ideas have been long brewing with him, and take some grasping first time out, I was still transfixed with interest and determined to stick with it.

Then I pulled out a question I could firmly stand behind, "Just what is it about going forward into the future?" Lewis replied, "It simply won't go! I can only reason that, in our continuum, there is no extension of the fourth dimension to any point that can be arrived at before we (and that includes our surroundings) can arrive at before the normal passage of time. Returning here in the forward time direction is different because it is travelling a route that is already mapped out in a sense. But then it won't go any further than present, and that natural buffer needs to be used, as I don't have a stop in the logic control in the forward direction. If I had to count it, I don't think I could reliably allow for lapsed time (or time away) anyway, and hey! If I was wrong, that would be a sticking point, and forever more perhaps." "Yes! I think I've got all that," I replied, and we left it at that for this session.

# CHAPTER THREE
FURTHER DEVELOPMENT – DEEPER IN

That evening, I got home in good time for the family meal, and at least this time my mother didn't give me the usual about not being sure that I'd join them until it was too late to lay a place and warm a plate for me. Though sure enough my father commented, "Was this a study day in your timetable Paul? Did the library close for a fire alarm or something?" My dad could only think that I would be studying when out of the house, maybe like he did and I often think he believes I am somehow differently motivated to the typical student he teaches. No ready thought that I might otherwise be socialising, more especially having an early evening drink at the college bar. "Anyway Tish, if he's in a daze", my father quipped, "it probably means they are working him hard, and there's nothing wrong with that for keeping a firm timely discipline in the mind."

So I dazed on, looking at my dad and wondering just what he would make of the ability to look back in history for real. It would be much more than just a supplement to his studies, but 'mum' is the word as they say. Then I thought more about Lewis, and that I would obviously go along with him. I am only pleased that I'll not be faced with the decision – what to do about it? The very thought of going public, no matter how carefully, gave me a shudder. "Cold Paul?" asked my mother. "A bit," I replied, "I walked up from the village centre, I met with the bus stop between bus times and didn't just want to stand." My mum looked, sympathetically as always, "As you've finished, take your drink through to the telly, the fires nice and high," she said. Shortly after I did so they joined me, and were soon away into the two-hour detective drama, leaving me to my preoccupying thoughts with the viewed backcloth of the fire flames.

Being aware of my full-on interest in this Lewis was still on a high himself when I saw him next day. After having talked more about it, effectively sharing his secrets with me, Lewis invited me to his house that weekend. He said his father was away at a show and he agreed to keep an eye on things, but of course this gave further privacy to our running of experiments.

A few days later the weekend came, after what seemed like a long time to my excited state of mind and we were in the barn, as Lewis was setting up. "I have had further thoughts," I said. "I hope by that you just mean further questions and not that you're gonna run off and quit on me," responded Lewis. "Oh of course, that's what I mean," I said, followed by a question, "is nothing left behind on the spot?" "In a way yes," replied Lewis, "but that takes further explanation, it's more like this spot is reserved. But I am going to show you something first of all in just a moment." Lewis continued to talk on after he stopped fiddling for a while. "Right then, I can move it relative to that position, again in multiples of one metre of further latitude which is straight forward, or by longitude with a side step of the charge combing by moving the polar spike once under way. All counted out on the presets with one metre 'quantisation intervals', to use what I now understand from our course to be the correct technical term for minimum definable units."

After doing something mysterious with an internal keypad in the probe, Lewis unhooked and retrieved the charging and video cables, then closed the panel which was evidently see-through to the camera. To my excitement and open-mouthed amazement, once I stood adjacent to him as he returned to the bench, the probe flashed on with a couple of arcs. It then shimmered with almost a rolling cloud affect in a very bright bluey-white. "You should really use these glasses," Lewis said as he handed me what looked like lab safety glasses blacked out, "you can just about get a 'welder's flash' from it at the start up stage." It then dimmed and even went sort of feint and less solid looking, and I understood from Lewis that this was because the eddy effect was starting to comb back the space. Then in the blink of an eye it disappeared. "Where's it gone?" I asked in layman's speak. "It's here," replied Lewis, "on this very spot, only Wednesday at this time. It'll be back again in this very place, or should I say 'in view' soon."

Sure enough, as Lewis confidently promised, the probe reappeared after about five minutes away and quickly turned back down to its cold metallic look. Lewis then busied himself with the connectors etc. "Is it hot to handle?" I asked. "No," said Lewis, "fair question, but I can only say that it is not the same as air friction, 'cos there is no direct contact layer with the surroundings. Even if you got it into the middle of a furnace, it wouldn't actually be in the middle of that environment it would be occupying this 'non-space' in that very geographical location." "I think I've got it," I said. "Anyway, look at this!" Lewis beckoned my attention to the TV ring and sat me in the centre chair. What I saw was this very area of the barn, with both of us walking back and forth and then over to the bench. "This was Wednesday," said Lewis, "we were here at about this time." "You could have just recorded that," I expressed as my reaction. "That wouldn't have been as easy," Lewis humoured, as he then started to switch the gear off again for the close of session on the night. We both then headed for a pint in the Farmer's Rest a couple of hundred yards down the road, following my suggestion and Lewis' agreement to mull things over a bit more.

As we walked in the evening air, I puzzled, "Why didn't we see it on Wednesday or at least know it was there?" "You are now getting into the philosophy," Lewis said. "The 'Time Paradox' – yes I read a bit on that," I replied. "Well," said Lewis, "it doesn't matter really. You see we had no prior knowledge of it, and we wouldn't sense it anyway." "The interspace?" I said looking for confirmation. Lewis nodded as we got to the pub door, saying that he wanted me to be aware though, that he had before now known the term 'interspace' referred to in the mobile phone industry, more specifically in marketing, for when they come into their own between offices as a tool to keep users working – making more use of travelling from a study called 'Time Geography'. I nodded in turn, as I could hardly respond with, 'what's in a name?' Knowing how I've been caught up about mine. From then, nothing more was said as we were very much in public now.

We sat close to the bar and I was mistaken by Lewis' expression of what I thought were the signs of a deep-thought look. But he was actually earwigging. He put his finger to his lips to confirm that I should sit quietly while he tuned in to two guys at the bar who evidently worked on the local river road tunnel. They still had their bright safety jackets on, bearing the tunnel logo, as they had called in for a pint after what had been an unusual delay in getting away from work. Lewis could hear them better than me as they were nearer his side of the table, and he looked a bit worried as he caught up with me on it later. It seems that they have a very precise linear movement sensing system in the tunnel. For movements and things like that that threaten its stability – instant location of cracks, or more like geological fault movements etc, and they had had an alert an hour or so earlier. He also heard them say that they had been fully assured by the instrument makers, that whilst the system had expected calibration limitations, it is within the levels accepted by the National Physical Laboratory and it would never give a false reading of movement. "It's really not much North of the same latitudinal path I have been using straight off from the farm here on the Boldon Flats," confirmed Lewis, with a simple reference to his A to Z he pulled out of his dad's truck door, as we walked back past his house gate. "I'll have to think some more about this," he said, "see you at Uni next week." Leaving him to his thoughts I cycled back along the lane, digesting what I'd just experienced in the cool night air.

When you're thinking that you've possibly encountered the most interesting thing in your life so far, you can't wait for more, it certainly fills your waking thoughts as well as your twilight sleep. Especially when you lie in bed with unease because of it, the time before you can get to it again seems like ages, it reminded me of Christmas Eve when I was a child. That's how it was with me in the early part of the following week. Indeed looking at some of the studies made and philosophy of time, it does explore the view that when one is anxious, worried, or excited about an event, then time goes more slowly than when one is relaxed and of a happy disposition. As is said, 'time flies when you are enjoying yourself' and this is an understandable psychological aspect of relative time, which ranges from this to the decelerated passage of time when in danger performing some life threatening manoeuvre.

Anyway, at the same scene again of the family meal table, my dad was boning me about being preoccupied when he suddenly said, "Did you see those official looking guys around the campus today, especially round your science block?" He knew that I hadn't by the surprised look I returned him, but I would rather he thought that I simply hadn't been in than having had some background worries about anything sounding like an investigation. "What would they want there?" I asked. "It'll no doubt come up at the next interdepartmental meeting, which I believe is Wednesday this week, to be at least minuted as an activity of the month. I think it's likely to be the United Kingdom Energy Authority, who are the watchdogs for fissile material and for that they reserve the right to make unannounced visits. We may well see them more often these days with the national security concerns."

On Wednesday night my father came home through the front door, swinging his hat on to the stand saying, "Well Paul, the visit was mentioned and this time it happened to be representatives from the National Physical Laboratory. However, I would have thought they'd be more the white coated types only, whereas the group I saw looked more like the 'Men in Black' in the films. Although when the UKEA guys have been they seem to have minders too, I think that's some branch of the Transport Police. All of these Civil Authorities probably all need some support in case of a sticky situation."

The very mention of the National Physical Laboratory gave me a sickening feeling of concern over what was said by the Tunnel guys. My mind then extrapolated to the thought that they must be poking around the area to look into the detected distortion, and with some inkling of course, they would go to the nearest lab, which could have some conceived capability, such as the Uni. But they can't be happy to have drawn a blank. With these thoughts building up, I couldn't wait to caution Lewis about it, and I would be seeing him normally enough next day. No need for any panicky flapping action though, everything needs to be cool; we don't want to raise any suspicion.

Next day came, and Lewis walked straight over to me. I never was very good at hiding worries facially, when sure enough he asked, "What's up then?" Followed with, "I know – the visitors, I've looked into it directly." I listened with all ears as Lewis explained that he'd sent the probe into the operations room of the National Physical Lab, the organisation he remembered the tunnel guys had mentioned, and had it sitting there for a couple of days, with the full expectation that any sensor pick up would knowingly be discussed there. He then brought back the recording as usual and was able to see quite a lot revealed on the display board around the discussion groups. "Without being an expert you can lip-read readily some of what was said – quite clearly really," said Lewis. "But yes the authorities are definitely out looking and any college Physics department is a sensible place to start," he added. "My dad confirmed who the guys were around campus, but without anything from me to start the issue," I said, "although I did nod on the prompt for him to take up the question at his latest interdepartmental staff meeting."

Lewis looked at me long and hard, and then said, "I take on board the view you first imparted to me, that you see your dad as a considerate and ethical man, and of course in his position he is well connected in the academic world." I confirmed furthermore by saying, "Certainly the 'academic world' of historians, and he is a media consultant for TV documentaries and politicians, or more correctly their researchers." Lewis mustn't of thought that I was just about to run dry with my 'dad-wise' complimentary appraisal, when he dived straight in at that point with, "What I am really getting to Paul is that he is trustworthy, he is a noted historian, and as such is the very sort I had in mind with my developments. Also as he no doubt has selective official connections, I think we should bring him into our confidence – what do you think? Mind you, before you answer, I have heard it reasoned that the chances of keeping a secret, is halved by every extra person. It was in some murder book I think, illustrating that the only watertight way was only for the murderer to know." We could both readily see the parallel in that.

"Yes, I am sure that would be okay," I said, "any gripe I've got with my dad is more of a relative age and acceptance of adulthood thing. I can say without doubt though, that he is a man who puts integrity well above notions of personal gain and all that." "Anyway have a think about it," said Lewis, "I'll expect you to tell him if you feel it right, that's my level of trust in you."

Well, I felt really boosted by that as I walked home that day, doing so to give myself healthy exposure to the light breeze of the afternoon, to blow away the tension and to have time to collect my thoughts. Hope I can catch dad on a receptive footing as well as his usual studious one. I convinced myself that I could firm up the required link from Lewis' to my dad's interest. If I was more suspicious in nature I might obsess a little more over how this came about. But then I am fully convinced that mine and Lewis' meeting could be nothing more a chance coincidence that is working out for the good. After all, I befriended him, not the other way around and so if I do have any insight, it tells me that he is a genuine guy.

# CHAPTER FOUR:
## THREE-WAY INVOLVEMENT

So back at our kitchen table again - whilst we did have a formal dining area, along with a lot of our contemporaries with a fast daily living, we have slipped into the habit of using it for Christmas, or for the sake of guests. Though it is a useful way to be, as more generally my mother likes to keep on the hop between the table and the appliances, and in that respect just sits readily with her apron on in preparation for the next serving. This is her preference, for she sees that quite sensibly as extended use of clothing protection, and disregards any suggestion this may have of classic role modelling. She is simply often cooking before getting changed out of her day clothes. She has an interest in cooking and food, which she enjoys almost as much as her flower beds and propagators, and in this she has developed some noted expertise – her understanding and examples of Mendelian Ratios came in handy for my biology schoolwork on genetics, I remember. Mum also has a liking for a daily soak in the bath for a full wind down after the evening meal, followed by a period of telly, whilst wearing her bathrobe as her relaxation attire. At least that's what we are used to on a weekday.

"Sitting here already Paul," she asked looking over at my pose of contemplation, i.e. head in hands, "it's going to be another half an hour yet, I am lining it up for when your dad's coming in, he said six on the phone." "That's okay," I said, "give me those peas and I'll shell them here for you on the table before we set it."

"Six o'clock and all's well!" I could hear my dad shout as he came through the door, and then he quipped, "I always did fancy the old job of Town

Crier. Mind you there is no news to speak of today, the networks must be having an AGM or something." He sat down to eat, and then when he sat back a bit and slowed from his initially ravenous behaviour, I postulated to him, "As an historian dad, what would you do if you could go back and see events for yourself?" There was a moment of silence. "As an historian, I might firstly be concerned about my job becoming redundant," he humoured, "and well, apart from not being able to do much about that 'tide of progress', there would be the need to be very selective. After all the total number of events over amassed history could be infinitely large. That is it could take you a lifetime to witness just a few, if you did them fully and in real time. Take the two World Wars for example – that's ten years, and say the first on its own - where would you spend it? On the Front, or in the Houses of Parliament? The choice is too wide and you would certainly want to witness major events." "In that respect I suppose you'd have the advantage of hindsight," I added. "One thing needs to be certain," he went on, "and that is that you must only observe, your presence must in no way alter anything. If you went back and had a job for instance, one which otherwise someone else would have done, you don't know what difference it may start as a chain of events." "Well!" I exclaimed, "I didn't expect such a considered response, you've obviously reasoned some of this out before dad." "Yes, 'I am not as green as I am cabbage looking' when it comes to a bit of logical reasoning, if I say so myself, and it can be quite stimulating really," he said. My mother, immediately and with perfect timing added, "I don't know though, he couldn't check the electricity bill against the meter dials the other day." "As I told you, that is not my field my dear," he replied in his defence as we all laughed.

"Anyway," he said, "to conclude this discussion, keeping away from current affairs as we've missed the six o'clock news tonight, let's take our wineglasses into the study and we shall talk some more Paul." Mum indicated she was happy with us stepping out like that, as she was waiting for our neighbour to return something, and it gave her an opportunity to 'chin-wag' away from the door with some welcome peer female company. This would be as part of her unwinding of the day, or more like 'downloading' I read it was for women, to enable them to relax – a cheeky comment perhaps, but then it seems to hold up with social research and what I have witnessed.

"So to round off the view I would take as a responsible time traveller," dad continued to say as we walk through and entered the study, "the view I take is that it is a bit like you see on the wildlife, or so called 'natural history' films. Where the cameraman is present when the big creature kills and eats the little creature, or the male lion kills the cubs of another male. As passionate people we feel we can easily change the outcome of what we are about to witness, but in principle we should certainly not interfere. Though when I say that, the only time I think I could justify action is when the very existence of the human race is a stake, where someone's mistake is leading to Armageddon." Then as we moved to sit down I affirmed, "As I say, what you express is well considered and I can't fault it." Hearing him talk like this warmed me to what I was about to reveal, as I said in a lowered tone, "I am glad its just us dad, 'cos I know you can be confidential and I need to go further with this, as I am now involved in something." "I am all ears!" He said using a common family expression and I could see he meant it as he gave me his full attentive gaze.

"I am pleased we have some wine, as my nerves have been getting to me over this. Partly through sheer excitement and partly through worry about some of the attention we've been getting," I confided. Then I continued after a deliberate pause, "What I am about to explain is that time exploration is definitely possible, for I've seen it done. Going back in time only and I don't mean time travel of passengers. Those events are more of science fiction, though to be fair we may say that we just don't know how to do it yet. However, there are sound physics principles around why we are only able to take it as far as we can." I then paused, prepared for my father's reaction, which may have been one of ridicule. Then I jumped in just before this anticipated response with, "And just to continue to promote an open minded approach here, going back in time which we now know is possible, cannot logically exclude travelling, or certainly probing here from our future, because of course that would be the present time of the time machine operator."

Dad thought he would share his knowledge to show he was interested, "I've read in one of the broadsheet science columns that there are theoretical views on curved space, like a sheet folding back on itself." While he fished through what he could recall of the article, I helped out with, "Or even a mobious band, where it has an twist so that both 'surfaces' (if we can say that of universal space) are outside and inside. The curved space idea allows progression around the curve in normal time, which can then be short cut straight through." "Wormholes!" He exclaimed. "Yes, but a direct link to our future in this way means that you still need somehow to accept that the future position will already be there, mapped out. Philosophically, this does not allow for our free will, and that's just one sticking point," I replied. "Even when you get a fast traveller, something proven in a small way by a round the world jet, and the time having slowed relative to an earth bound twin clock, that is not 'travelling into the future' as such. Logically this is because, at the same starting point, which you have to take - whenever, the commonly experienced future would not be there ahead of anyone making that future." "Funnily enough," dad said, "your mother is a great believer in 'fate'." "Well, I wouldn't want to disappoint her, but I need to say to you that there is little science in that." Dad could then recall more, as it was a recent article, but all the same he does have a good memory for names, "Also I read that a guy called Mallett is working on deliberately curving space on a lab scale with lasers to prove the principle." I am used to my dad, throwing things in like this, testing my argument I suppose. So then I felt must round off with the comment, "He may well get somewhere, but that doesn't say it is the way it is for us, and as I am saying to you this is something that works!"

All in all in after hearing this tall story, or more like incredible tale, dad just sat back looking to the ceiling. Then turned to me with a slight smile and gave a semi-serious comment, "Well, I know its not April 1st, and I know you don't go in for that sort of carry-on anyway." I smiled as I asked him which afternoon we could meet together early leaving the Uni site, with the idea that we could go to a prearranged session at Lewis' lab in the early evening. With a surprisingly simple response, he just nodded cooperatively, and so I just kept the mood light by saying, "We'll bring home fish and chips to save the time of a cooked meal so we can get a start."

Agreeing on next Wednesday after consulting his diary, which he had to hand in his briefcase, dad then said, "Tell me more, you've got me hooked now!" So I continued, "I am not sure of everything, as it's my friend Lewis who developed it, and it's he who we will meet with on Wednesday. You'll realise the venue when we arrive. We're getting more twitchy about how much can be revealed etc." "Understood," said dad, "but can I ask for now, what were you saying about the physical limitations?"

"Well it's a probe rather than a vessel," I replied, "it cannot transport anything, and certainly we don't think that anything biological will survive, but then there would be no point as it is not possible to breech the spatial fold that the probe lies within when it is outside of its own time. It was explained to me that it is effectively an infinitely thin chamber, between space, invisible to the observer outside of it who looks around and past it rather than through it. It is not possible to pick up sound, scent, or convected heat as there is no molecular interchange. Lewis is not altogether sure of radiated heat, as of course he records images which means that the electromagnetic spectrum is involved, but he needs to explore wavelengths further beyond the visible spectrum. If Lewis could be more sure that it would be okay, he was speculating over witnessing the very first atomic explosion. It would certainly survive the 'blast' as far as it is a violent rush of air but there's uncertainty about radiated heat. After all the circuits are just normally tolerant components −50 degrees up to +120 degrees to physically work and come back unscathed. But then the recording mechanics won't give of their best anywhere near those limits, and as recording is the purpose, there is no point without." "I am absolutely amazed," dad responded, "it would be a fantastic tool for historical certainty. You've got me exited now, and that takes some doing in an old man."

With that we laughed and agreed to say no more until Wednesday's evening meeting of what has now become the involved three, which I trust will become a collaboration of three. Even though my dad had been surprisingly light hearted so far, I knew him well enough as a matter-of-fact man, and realised that he would probably just be happier to find out for himself, as to whether this was real or imaginary.

Wednesday came and then we did as planned in the late afternoon. The arrangements couldn't have worked out more suitably, mum was happy to have some takeaway food delivered by us which she rushed, as she had now set-up a night over at a friend's Tarot-card reading, I think she said. Anyway, with her not planning to be back until ten we could have an easy three to four hours with Lewis. As my dad said agreeably, when we were out of earshot, "The simpler the better – the fewer explanations made the better, or as they used to say in war in an attempt to keep convoy movements as unknown as practicable, 'loose lips sink ships'."

I began to appreciate my dad a bit more, he seemed to have the balance just right between the light hearted - don't know what to expect but anything goes - non-suspicion drawing approach and the serious/ confidential attitude we three will need to maintain.

I kept quite quiet on our way over in dad's car, wanting to hold more of a wait-and-see standpoint on what can be quite a mind-bending concept. But dad was quite happy to go on excitedly and state what his ambitions would be if he could observe any earth bound event retrospectively, "You could go back to the scene of any crime – you could confirm the identity of Jack the Ripper, or who shot Kennedy. You could check out the Scriptures – loaves and fishes, walking on water, or the parting of the Red Sea."

Then as we arrived, I could see that some closed circuit TV cameras had been fitted to the farm out buildings nearer the main road, as they swivelled to follow us. Lewis then came out to meet us and swept over the car with one of those clothes brush like search wands they use in court. Fortunately the only bugs coming in with dad's car were on the windscreen. "Can't be too careful nowadays," remarked Lewis, "just want to show you that I am taking this seriously." His actions were coupled with a half kidding smile, as he lead us into the barn and further through to his equipment. "Anyway," as he turned and looked up putting his kit back on the bench, "it's a pleasure to have you here Professor Stapleton." "Thank you whole heartedly for involving me," was the reply, "and just so we are off to the open trusting start we want, you don't need to use the formal title. After all we are officially only supposed to be Professors or Doctors in academic formality or Identity Documents." "Well actually," said Lewis, "with you both having 'Paul' in your first names, when it comes to calling out instructions as a team it may well be best to call you 'Prof.' leaving Paul as he is." "Okay, I'll go with that," said dad. "Good then Prof." I said, then dad turned to me with a smile and a waggly finger, "only here will I let you away with that, in the interests of efficiency, not at home where I should continue to admit that I know you as my son."

From that simple icebreaker we all laughed. Then dad (Prof) went straight in with a question, "Lewis could I just ask you, taking on board everything dutifully explained by Paul so far, and accepting that I haven't experienced or witnessed anything yet, is there a risk that the probe might come out in the middle of a solid object or somebody – quite literally?" Why didn't I think of that, was my unoriginal thought. "Paul may have explained," answered Lewis, "you just need to grasp that it makes it way back through the fourth dimension of time by 'combing' the other three dimensions of space past itself." "It sort of accumulates negativity in space/time, if you prefer to see it that way quantitatively," I contributed wishing to sound informed. "Well it may be fortunate then," dad replied, "that I'm from the earlier generations that weren't seen as leaving school successfully unless they could add up and have competency in quantitative methods (sums), even if they weren't choosing a career in science or engineering." "Anyway, directly to your very good question," said Lewis specifically directing himself then at dad (Prof), "what I can only believe happens is that the object or person folds around it so to speak. So that in the 'middle' of a person, or more correctly a person's coincident space you would probably see just a full screen set here of green colouring, say if they wore a green jacket." As Lewis drew our attention to the tellies with a nodding gesture, "Giving a 360 degree image around them, we need to conceive of a 360 degree-ish covering envelope of said person. As the probe when outside of its own original time/space occupies an infinitely thin cylinder of in-between-space, then said person walking around the floor say, would flow around it imperceptibly." "Unlike what you might think of as walking smack centre into a band saw," I said to contribute an illustration. "Yes I am with it so far as long as you're in the realms of conceptual thinking, and you don't get too technical on me," said dad as he looked across at both of us. I felt it as a lifting moment as here dad was for the first time that I had known, admitting, although indirectly, that I may actually know or understand the detail of something that he doesn't. I seized my chance, albeit in front of Lewis, and spoke out with, "Another thing that takes a bit of grasping is that it only really belongs where it is. You can move it conventionally as we are in space, in normal time as the clock ticks by, but once movement is in time or in time and space then it cannot belong anywhere else, and for the balance of universal forces its correct 'space' is here and now." "Just one correction," said Lewis, "when you say time or time and space, it will always be time and space. Because to arrive back here say, yesterday, then it will have been around one full orbital set of spaces in order to return. Then in line with what you say it cannot occupy its own space twice. That is both yesterday proper and yesterday's visit from today at the same time." "Goodness knows what would happen if there wasn't 'Interspace' then," I replied.

"Dare I admit?" Dad followed on, "it may just be too technical for me, though I see your not going to send it tonight Lewis, as you've got the 'bonnet-up' as it were." "No but I'll show you an example recording it made," said Lewis as he directed us to the viewing chair, "it's best if you've got a fairly precise time as well as an exact place for an event obviously. There's one I would like to have shown you, but I seem to have a spoiled disc. You'll no doubt be aware of the Loch Ness Monster, and then there was the most famous 'Surgeon's photo' of the head and neck. I went back to the scene and witnessed an accomplice of his putting what looked like a plastic model just off the shore for him to photograph. It was something which the model handler (and maker) exposed on his deathbed when he was around ninety – some sixty years later. The Doctor had long since died abroad, where he had gone to avoid any more exposure. No doubt it grew bigger than they had both expected. The confession was that it had been a hoax as well as describing his methods with a model submarine and a fashioned stuck-on head, and sure enough there they were on the recording. Shortly after the confession, the museum at Drumnadrochit changed its commercial symbol from a facsimile of said photo to a logo version, in disassociation. I wanted to take it up and review other sightings, and I may still do that yet, but again it could only be for self interest in a conclusion."

"Hey mind, Lewis!" I spoke out with what I hoped would be an impressive contribution, "it might be a problem area - 'geographical area' I mean, because 'time slips' have been offered as possible explanations of the sightings. That they are not there in real time at all, but those observers have been seeing a distant past event. Really suggesting that the Great Glen fault and its side slippage along a north-eastern line is some sort of spatial-warp. Also, as far as I know, there are no sounds of splashes or cries reported adding to its plausibility." Lewis all the while had been preparing while we were talking and was now ready.

With my father sitting attentively in the chair, and me holding the back as if I was a Waltzer operator about to give him a spin, Lewis then replayed a recording which I recognised straight away as the young Albert Einstein. He was in a small gathering that looked like a friends dinner party. Lewis then explained what we should see: "The view on the most part has always been that Einstein was a brilliant mathematician – he is even deferred to in the expression 'I am no Einstein'. Well it turns out that really he possibly couldn't have altogether lived up to that alone. As I fast-forward, what you see here as the discussion breaks up and the friends leave, is the great contribution made by his first wife, Mileva Maric. You'll recognise those formulations Paul that she is noting and some of the other documents placed on the table. But unfortunately I haven't been able to pick up on the famous summary $E = mc2$. I do think though that it obviously shows her mathematical ability for working through the concepts, as it is her notation being produced right there. Concepts which are fully accepted as his, as he was a great 'lateral thinker', even though he may have sounded them off his academic friends at such homely evening gatherings.

It was not like the present time for female recognition. To be taken up by the scientific establishment, ideas had to be presented by a man. Marie Curie had a similar resistance to break through, and there were others. Around that time in Nuclear Fission was Lise Meither." "They should be kindred thoughts to dad here," I added, "'history' of science." Lewis replied to that, and said, "I have always followed through on the history of any concepts I need to deal with, almost as a matter of course, as I find it greatly helps my understanding. There are many unsung heroes, then more so as 'the under-recognised' there are heroines, and that can be a subject in itself. It's not my field, but there was also Rosalind Franklin and Dorothy Hodgkin from Crystallography and Biochemistry/ microbiology, and nearer to the Scientific Renaissance was the work done on physics mechanics by a mathematically talented aristocrat called Emilie du Chatelet. Oh yes, and an unpublished research paper on mosses and lichen was withdrawn on the grounds of sexism in the scrutinising committee by one Helen Beatrix Potter, then a noted Botanist at the turn of the 19th century. She then found her fame as we know in children's literature." In contribution, I said, "I remember seeing something on her first story about Peter Rabbit, that it was pulled together from something she constructed in letters to a sick child who was a close relation, and 1893 comes to mind – dad here always made sure I at least read from the greats, even as a youngster." "Of course now I could easily get an evidence record of their contributions," concluded Lewis.

Dad was quietly engrossed, and then spoke as he shook his head in awe, "That's amazing Lewis and what potential! Images from one hundred years ago. The only thing I am readily aware of with Einstein, is that he was offered the Presidency of Israel, and was promised that he could continue with his scientific work 'without interruption', but he declined. Seventy-three years old at the time." Lewis added, "He published three 'world changing' papers in 1905. This was certainly the height of someone's powers. Yet at the time he was only known to a small circle of specialists, getting publicity almost fifteen years later from some New York Times exposure on 10th November 1919. He lived mainly on the reputation of that early work until he died in 1955, not doing anything as great after Mileva left the scene. The Universal Field Theory that he was 'working' on remained largely unfinished, and it is known that he had a mathematician called Straus helping him then, though understandably he may have 'blunted his pencil with age' as it were. Of course the U.F. idea has since been reviewed, and the consensus is that Einstein was on the wrong trail with that one." "Save for your efforts here Lewis," I felt I must point out, "if that's not demonstrating the relationship between electromagnetism and gravitational space, I don't know what would?" "It is said," dad added, "that Isaac Newton had arguably the greater scientific mind, but the absence of twentieth century media has not left him as well celebrated." "Also there's Michael Faraday," I interjected, "and common to all three of them, was the motivation to understand and document the mechanisms underlying God's creation work on the world and the universe beyond. That's quite unlike the present day Stephen Hawking who unqualifyingly states his atheism, and yet something is keeping him going with his work on these forefronts, against the odds of his openly shown illness. Some may see that type of strength as somewhat spiritual."

Lewis then thought he had better lighten the philosophising hi-brow stuff with a quotation, as well as he could remember it, from a short verse in Punch, printed at the heady Einstein days: "There was a young lady quite bright, who travelled around the speed of light. She started one day in the relative way and returned the previous night." We could all see something of our situation in that and freely laughed.

Dad then sighed and turned, "So anyway lads d'ya fancy a pint next door, I'll buy – I certainly need something to wash down those heavy concepts, or should I say 'mind blowing' stuff, if that is more of a hip term these days?" "Yes, I think that a relaxing drink would be good for us all, thank you Prof," replied Lewis as he moved to turn down the lights.

We walked without talking down the road to the pub, individual reflection perhaps, but there was only the sound of crunching footsteps on the recently regritted surface. My reflection was to wonder just what dad's mind had made of Lewis' work. With that pub visit came the first time I had my dad sitting opposite me with a pint in a bar, certainly for any social alcohol consumption. The only other time I can recall is at family occasions to ease the formality. Furthermore this time he bought us two rounds. "He doesn't get out much," I light heartedly remarked to Lewis as dad was away buying. On his return to our table that we'd deliberately picked in an isolated corner, carrying only a half for himself, he said, "I am driving remember! Anyway you might think there aren't many tongue loosing liquids quite like real ale, when I say to you that you guys certainly have my confidence and my confidentiality. I am feeling that I should fully accept what you say without a demo so far. After all I don't see why anyone in your respective positions would invent a story, and it's got to be a wasted effort if it were a confidence trick. I mean in my reasoning Lewis, that it would not be me as a first choice for any such a thing as a research grant in my official capacity of having a say over Humanities Department funds, when other organisations could be paying telephone numbers towards some technical projects. Straight forwardly, it's got to be easier to invent the thing than to fabricate a story with visual affects etc." Dad raised his eyebrows as if expecting confirmation. "Mind I don't know?" Lewis said after a momentary lull, with a put on man of mystery smile which became quite infectious, and with that I could see we were all going to get along fine.

I then thought I would take a little risk with dad during this get to know each other chat and let him out a bit, to show that he too can be wrong, by telling Lewis that he wondered about G.P.S. for a moment. That is until I pointed out that there would be a very limited number of years coverage. "Yes, ok Paul," he uttered, "and if I was to make an excuse, it might be that it would not be obvious to the uninitiated." "Well, we'll just have to get the 'initiation' over as soon as possible," commented Lewis, in keeping with the mood, "and a less obvious problem with GPS would be 'traceability'. Not to mention charges as well, for I wouldn't like the result from reckoning up the bill we would have, from how much use it would register." "- And that in itself may get you readily 'overdue' bills!" I exclaimed, to laughs all round.

"Just for clarity on this point though folks, assuming our 'thinking caps' have slipped too far to the side tonight," said Lewis, "any resultant positioning errors in its spatial-jump counting would tend to increase with increased length of journey. Although having said that, my experience so far in the 'near region' has been actually so slight as to be hardly perceptible, but as it happens, accuracy and precision needs themselves work away with 'the years'." "Of course," dad said, as he cottoned straight on to that, "built up areas with dense structures exist relative to now, whereas much earlier times had sparser populations and more open settlements with activities less fixed, allowing for exceptions like Roman forts." "Exactly," said Lewis, "positioning reliability is less of an essential feature, and I was tempted just then to say 'as time goes by' but that infers the wrong direction." That remark also got a laugh. Lewis then rounded off the point by saying, "It does return as a matter of course with the same pattern in reverse (errors included). So arrival back to us is to the same N/S-E/W co-ordinates, and in practice, the same spot within the dedicated/marked area on the barn floor."

This point got dad and I to the bottoms of our glasses, so we made a move to leave, then Lewis quickly finished his and joined us for a brisk walk back, including some unrelated polite chat, until we parted. "That was a real buzz," I said to dad after he let me into the car, and after assuring me that that wasn't such a new expression, he acknowledged that he felt the same. Neither of us felt the need to say any more that day, and for that matter, said little more that week. Such experiences and facts do take a lot of digesting!

# CHAPTER FIVE:
## BACKING OFF

The following week I was sitting in the student union café-bar one lunchtime on my own having a sandwich, when I saw my father walk across the floor towards me looking somewhat stern faced. "What, brings you here then amongst us plebs – is the staff canteen closed?" I asked. "Well, fortunately no-one is going to be suspicious of me talking to my own son in his break time, but that is the problem," as he lowered his voice. Then he said, "Suspicion could well pose a problem, we need to meet together, the three of us again. Your lectures are finished at half-two today, you said this morning, I do remember. I have to see an allocated personal tutee now, but it should be brief." "Lewis is getting one of those sessions now," I interjected. Dad rolled his eyes in thought, looking reflective he said, "Best then if we talk in the study at home. Take Lewis there, I'll follow on, and we'll have enough time before your mother gets in." I wasn't able to do anything but nod, as I'd taken another big bite of the sandwich, but it was probably best to let him continue. He certainly seamed a bit flustered, coupled with nervously walking away which was a bit out of character.

Lewis came in by the time I'd finished my lunch. Then I went across to him in the queue and said quietly to his ear, "Something's up, we've got to go straight off. Grab a sandwich to eat on the way and a can to carry if you need a drink." With that we set off, knowing that dad would catch us by the time we got there as he was coming by car. Imagining directional microphones and allsorts of overhearing tools, feeling a bit spooked, I just said to Lewis, "I don't know anything really other than he is anxious to talk to us both, so I can only believe its our joint venture," as I raised my eyebrows to convey secret meaning. I also assured him that it would be as private as possible. Only three of us in a study, within a house with no one else in. It certainly could not be thought of as anything unusual for me to have a course colleague there, having a friendly word with my dad from the same college.

We no sooner got there and had the kettle boiled, when dad walked in, so as he took his coat off I carried the tea tray through to the study with the pot and three cups, Lewis holding the doors. "Right lads, let's wet our whistles before we start." Dad then sat down, scanned both of us and said further, "I am aware from a another senior staff meeting today that we have had some irregular contact from the DDA." Lewis looked knowingly at me and spoke up, "I saw that lettering in the recording made of the meeting with the National Physical Lab, what does it stand for?" Dad was a bit taken aback by what Lewis just said, but took it and then spoke on. "Well that's in line with my most cautious thoughts, it is the Defence Diversification Agency in Farnborough, which was set up in 1999 to promote cross-fertilisation of technology between UK defence labs and industry. It would seem quite acceptable in a peaceful world, but it doesn't take much cynicism to imagine that it can quite determinedly lean very much one way 'in the Public Interest'.

This time they addressed us together, in our exclusively Senior group, to say that they had evidence that there were momentary time slips being produced and an approximate triangulation lead them broadly to the North of England." Lewis felt he should re-confirm at this point for dad's benefit, the meeting he'd observed on the trip with the probe, that I had already been made aware of, which was directly to the investigator's offices. He then went on to say, "Yes, my 'witness' recordings if you like, did show a map of the sensors for the National Physical Laboratory's Time-Slip project. With what I worked out were the names and locations of major road tunnels, or more essentially, those well placed for attempts at triangulation. There was the Tyne, the

Clyde, the Mersey, and I think the Blackwall twin tunnels, down in London. In fact I am sure it was, because the twin tunnels had a sensor set-up each, and functioned with a deliberate gap. This was intended for their next refinement planned to complete it as a sensor ring, with each acting as a terminal, if you like, to the outer circuit of an almost classic-kite shaped net. I did in considering their first effort, wonder why the 'Chunnel' did not feature, after all it's the biggest one, but now I think it's this geographical network intention." "I also think you've hit on it with the title 'National'," said dad, "it takes quite a bit to get inter-'national' cooperation over anything scientifically or technically sensitive, especially with implications. Naturally nations want to find out for themselves, then keep as much to themselves as possible."

"Looks like there may be some method in the selection of sites," I thought aloud, "as they surround most of England's technological/ industrial capability as a geographical area, when you visualise it on the map. It would also seem to miss out major geological features, those more so of Wales and Scotland. These avoided locations themselves should make us a bit suspicious of their real intentions, that is to be as more a search for synthetic association with time-slips than natural perhaps?" "Well it is the DDA, not some geological or meteorological group, that's tied in on this investigation with the National Physics Laboratory," affirmed dad. "Physical," I said as I jumped in, almost primed to correct him at any opportunity, the way he always did with me on words, yet on the day it didn't give me any satisfaction. Dad continued, "In line with what you've just said about their developments Lewis, they were only able to say with approximation that the disturbance was within a geographical band, as they only knew it was between sensors. We can likely understand that to mean North of two and South of two. They said the detection was of momentary slippage in and out of state, that is, back to origin or datum in nanoseconds. This also affirmed that they were likely to have been artificially produced – a synthetic affect.

They then asserted that someone was maybe working on something that they do not know the full effects of at best, or at worst someone is working clandestinely, knowingly keeping it out of the public domain or academic domain and therefore any possible take up by the DDA.

I thought straight away of your work Lewis, but then I thought – what possible military use could a device that did not allow any involvement by direct interference with events be? Then it struck me! It's the penultimate spy tool, and I say that rather than ultimate, because it is after the event and cannot by its nature be actual time. It also has no sound recording, though that's not an obstacle to picking up close conversations by a good lip-reader, something which in the very least experts at spying would have in resource. Of course right now they don't know what they could discover without looking. What I am saying is, the view that we have to take is the one where they are fully aware, for us to have precaution. I expect that most of their needs would be essentially doing what you have done, witnessing meetings etc. I am as patriotic as the next man when it comes to defence, that's not to say I would step outside of our pact – at best I may try to persuade you both. But when it comes down to political gain rather than national interests of defence I am dead against it. For historical reasons, for example, I might like to know exactly what went on over the Iraq war from a political-historian's point of view. But the idea of a party presently in government stealing a march on the opposition or on the rest of us in order to keep themselves in charge of our lives, well that's something else. I can count on two hands how many honourable and ethical men there have been in political prominence, in the so called 'civilised' world." Lewis and I just sat quiet listening and in thought, but it was a proud moment for me to see dad holding such a challenging view - good on him - long may he keep his spurs.

Dad went further, "Something else, and I never did mention this to anyone Paul, so it's news to you as well. For the last few years, firmly within the time of the present government, Universities with science and technology research interests and advanced level capability such as ours, have what I can only describe as 'sleepers' working with those very departments, who masquerade as teaching staff and sometimes technicians. It depends on the access needed, but they are legitimately employed from interviews etc. and are as capable as anyone. Anyway these 'agents', for want of a better word, are reporting back anything of value and use to the government to meet its ends. After all communication technology has flown away and up in the last few years, with a couple of step changes that we are all bathed in. As you know, 'Communication and Information Technology is knowledge', and if you control said Comm. and I.T. then you are in control! I was sceptical about this 'agent' business and I thought that the guys who perpetrated it were the most paranoid of our conspiracy theorist staff members. That is until the DDA guy who was speaking alluded to the fact that they did not know of any 'official' work going on, or more confidently sounding like they knew there was not – meaning without saying, from 'inside' sources. My Science and Engineering opposite numbers, guys you both know and love, have always seen the DDA as independently fair-minded. Whilst that's acceptably true, you will always have that party political direction making of whoever is Secretary of State for Defence, and whatever he or the PM etc. want to use it for. It's in the nature of ambitious personalities in power I am afraid. All sold to the rest of us as the 'Public or Defence Interest'." Dad then paused to drink his cooler tea, then he poured another round of tea adding, "Then of course that's just our place, presumably they'll be raking over similar ground with the likes of Sheffield University, let alone others nearer here." At this point he said no more to allow us to digest the impact of what he had openly presented.

Lewis readily expressing his deduced thoughts then said, "Well if it has to stop, it has to stop! Pity it's right now though, I have just recorded something quite specific, and whilst it hadn't come out quite as conclusively as I'd hoped, I was going to show you both anyway – what does 22nd November 1963 mean to you?" "Oh! JFK of course," said dad with a pleased smile. "Yes", said Lewis nodding, "something I know you have an interest in from a remark of Paul's the other day. Yes indeed, it's Kennedy's assassination." As Lewis looked over at me to make sure I was staying with it, he continued, "But as I say it is not conclusive from just one short visit and from where I placed it, on the famed 'grassy knoll' itself. It gave no better view of the rather gruesome event, except to say that there was no indication of a shot from there, or at ground height. By that I mean that the gun was evidently above the 'target' and above the viewpoint. Also as we can't hear shots firing to count them, as the reported three, including one miss, I was hoping that the muzzle flash would be clear. But the image is small of that window in the depository building, and the relative brightness of the sunny daylight takes the average video contrast too far down to be clear of a visual count at all – 'tut'! The dynamic range of visual technology still has a long way to go to be as good as the natural eye." "All opportunities, including repeated attempts will be limited now," I supposed. Then a few minutes passed while Lewis and I, as if with choreographed movements, both continued sipping and rolling our hands round the tea mugs with elbows on our knees. All three of us by then had our thoughts steered towards the grim prospects from this point. It wasn't the way we wanted our future to look.

"So is it ready to send off Lewis?" I asked. "- And tonight if possible," dad added as he started to sit back now a bit more with his hands more firmly around a less hot mug, "Just about everything is expendable to those who see the gain as great enough. Not wanting to put the frighteners on as such, but I am sure you'll see there is no time like the present to 'move it out of the way' as it were in layman's terms." He also added as he gazed at both of us, as if we needed further affirmation,

"On mission! I mean, as a more agreeable term." We all understood that this was a quick answer for a hide away. Lewis responded, "Leave it to me, I'll program it as soon as I get to the farm. Last time you saw it recharging – it usually sits on the mains charger until it ready to go. But apart from that it was being degaussed, if you remember, they were the coils ringed around it, something I need to do in servicing it from time to time. No matter though, come down tonight, and we'll be ready for the off. No need to drive me down, I will benefit from the fresh air." "Do take my bike then," I said as he left, "it's at the back door, I can get it later, if we were to come down." Dad and Lewis both nodded with affirmation that we should follow on.

# CHAPTER SIX:
## OUT OF SIGHT – OUT OF MIND

"Best if this is our last gathering for a while Paul," said dad as we drove in through the farm gates, "all three of us like this I mean." "Sure," I replied in one word to make it brief. Lewis waived us right over to the shed with the car, wanting us to take the car right through this time. "Best if mum and dad don't see your dad," he said at my window, "they'll wonder what he's here for, whereas you could be just a mate who pops in and out. I could give them a tale if we are seen, but the simpler our involvement the better." As the car was now out of view of the farmhouse, we were able to just get straight out and join him at the open barn door.

Lewis spoke as he walked us through the barn rooms, "There'll be two periods of 'detectability' we might say, first outward and then the eventual return, having any possible trace to here. This is to assume for the worst that such an exact trace were possible, and if not now, then we will have to assume that it will be in a year or more when it comes back. For now it'll be out the way for a good while as prescribed, and if we feel that they are on to us, we'll just have to be quickly organised in removing it as a last piece of evidence as soon as it arrives." He then got to the control bench with all panels on, and turned again to face us saying, "I'll go through what I have set up, bearing in mind that we don't have a lot of time to debate choices, but I can still make changes.

So then, I have it going back to Hiroshima, at exactly 'ground-zero'." "Mmm," said dad, "speaking purely historically, it's the centre of the four square miles of destruction, beneath the two thousand foot air burst of 'Lean Boy'," he winked at me, "see still got a quick memory for facts – not bad for an old man eh!" Then looking over at Lewis, who smiled and nodded, "If you don't mind me continuing," said dad, "now that I'm on a roll with the educational bit. The first one was Uranium235, and whilst the second 'Fat Boy' was Plutonium with an expected greater destruction, quite the opposite results turned out. Nagasaki was a substituted target and with different terrain, it was well populated with two hundred and fifty thousand, but then thirty-five to forty thousand were known killed or missing. Compared to twice as many in Hiroshima, at eighty thousand known killed plus ten thousand missing. Of course the numbers do not include those whose lives, including future lives of their offspring, were shortened by injury and exposure." "On that," added Lewis, "I have only just looked this up, and I saw it quoted as one hundred and forty thousand lives lost to the bomb on Hiroshima, all told." Dad nodded with a stern face of acceptance saying, "So in terms of events to witness, you've picked the greatest carnage of any single man made strike in history, as well as the first of only two uses of atomic bombs as weapons – quite a choice!" I was immediately struck by the gruesomeness of this, but then I could empathise with my dad's trained historian approach, by seeing that if we are able to know more about what it was like there, we should, and as it is we cannot alter the facts. So I contributed to reinforce a documentary style of discussion, "I've heard the bombs referred to as 'Little Boy' and 'Fat Man'." Acknowledging my question, dad said, "So have I. You'd think that there would be more certainty about something like that, so much for code names. But now we know Lewis has invented a historical controversy-solving tool... and you know something else with a twist, in more ways than one, it's the famously named 'Peace Dome', which is readily believed to be an old church. In fact it's the roof of a showroom within a previously insignificant industrial complex built in 1914."

"Well," continued Lewis, "it's going back to 05/04/45, and I've set a segmented few hours of recording of some months before, whilst they go through their Spring and up to their high and humid Summer months. A fuller recording on the day itself of 06/08/45, which I really see as more of an endurance test, and then during the after events. Taking it up to when they started to clear the roads in preparation for reconstruction, well up into late 1946 before it moves on." I then thought aloud, "For an endurance test of this sort, we might think that you could have sent it back purely to a bomb test site, but inline with what I believe of your approach to this dad, there would be no additional social/human history element to that." "Unless you mean Australia where the safety of Aborigines was not a feature," dad commented.

Lewis moved on to say, "So as this is, I need the recording times to be brief to ensure it's not out of energy. But it does need to be away in accumulated time (total days away) to come back at a planned time. Also as I explained to Paul before now, for a fail-safe it'll journey back when it has only enough stored energy to do so, and we don't want it turning up unexpectedly the way things are for us now. The reason for this built in safe guard as you might expect, is also because there is no other means of retrieval. We can't go and get it, and of course we simply don't know the longer term universal physics of something being permanently out of its established space/time. Too dangerous a step when we've nothing certain to rely on, it has to be firmer than any hypothesis" "- And as to Hiroshima - tell us more, what about the destruction event itself as far as the probe's survival goes, Lewis?" I asked. He replied, "As I see it, it's 'play or bust'. A good time to test my theoretical belief that it will be unaffected. If so we have new knowledge, if not it's a rebuild!" "Quite," said dad, "you could say 'knowledge' either way, and it's a good time to go for it faced with our situation." Admitting now, I for one did have a worry here but didn't express it, as I almost immediately refreshed my view with the confidence I had in Lewis. Accepting that he must believe in only two outcomes – recovery (i.e. return), or obliteration, nothing in between.

Lewis then added, "And that's not all, I am trying the multiple destination program routine. In this case a double journey with a call by at NASA's main meeting room for 09/06/69 – again with segmented recording over a period, using the 'animated presence trigger' this time (wasteful to record if there's no-one in)." "I know what you after there," I said, "the 'did we go to the moon' question." "Exactly," said Lewis. "Believed to have been on the 20th July U.S. time, or if I haven't confused myself with the recording around the expected event, it was also the 21st our time, as it happened around the flip-over at midnight." "Two good choices of historical significance," affirmed dad, and with that Lewis then proceeded to set things in motion, explaining for our benefit and a deliberate sharing of control, what he was switching/pressing and why.

Dad then became Lewis' second witness to the colourful and dramatic visuals from the probe as it disappeared. "Another number for you then guys, it all adds up to coming back here on Thursday 05/05/05. That's the number seen on Subaru rally cars '555' that I remember from when they were round near here, heading to and from the Kielder forest stage, and they were also the regular winners then," said Lewis. "Good," I said, "but it must have been some time ago 'cos the '555' was one of those sponsoring cigarette logos." "Well," replied Lewis, "I must confess to having within my interests more of a catalogue of tractors than cars. I mean how else could I get a Lamborghini from £21K, or more unexpectedly a Ferrari from £14K.

Anyway I'd planned that all three would be easy to memorise 5445, 9669, and now 555," concluded Lewis, "meanwhile I'll put things under wraps and remove those authority meeting recordings so far, unless you would both like to see them?" In response to Lewis' look, I looked left and right to both of them saying, for dad's benefit, "To make any sense of them we have to view them here in the 360 degree projection." "Well no then," dad replied, "I don't need it to firm up my trust on all on that has been said. Though I do say I am only unaffected by saying 'no' to such a recent recording of a couple of meetings, and maybe not to historic highs full of mystery and controversy - maybe next series." He smiled and so did Lewis, saying, "Good! That way no tie-ups or incriminating evidence. Lab and video equipment as it is here, is legitimate enough for an Applied Physics student/Instrument Technician."

"Well here's to 555 then," concluded dad, "not meaning anything superstitious by it, but as Paul knows, I am 55 in 2005 on the following June 20th." "Eleven years to go then," summised Lewis. "Maybe just one," replied dad, "as I have an option of early retirement, and I had thoughts on using it to get away from academic administration, government targets for hoop jumpers and all that, into the real purpose of my background that is, to add to the educational value of historical writing. Mind you I hadn't anticipated, with any sense of realism a device which would remove assumption or conjecture. Not that I intend to over this, but it would also be good to be free of any sense of obligation to report 'findings' to the academy." "The very purpose I had in mind," said Lewis as he reached out to shake hands with dad by gentlemen's agreement." I then over-clasped my hand on theirs saying, "We'll see then, we'll do this again!"

With broad nods we made a move toward parting, with dad saying, "Next June will give you two a chance to stick to the curriculum through to your second year end. Then Paul you have your 'Industrial Placement' and it might be possible to do this down-on-the-farm, if I can suggest, under the aegis of Lewis' agricultural engineering repair business." Lewis shrugged and nodded as if willing to be flexible, so dad then turned back and continued, "I am sure you could both swing it. Not that it's the way I operate, but this I am sure is for the greater good, so I'll see if I can pull a retirement favour to have you both approved for it. That way we could have a year's worth of intense activity." "Or more," I said, "we would have from June to the following year's end of September/ beginning of October." Lewis just nodded in broad agreement. Dad then offered, "I'll check the start up dates for what will then be the relevant 'semesters' rather than 'term times' – that's another reason to go, we are being further Americanised." Lewis and I laughed, and dad and I then left him to the mothballing of the equipment himself, in the self-trusting meticulous way he preferred.

As my father and I walked back and then into the car he said, "If we were to get things up and running again purposefully, we'd have to get away from the mainland detectors." "What about the Isle of Man then?" I said off the cuff. "So your thinking of me as a tax exile then," answered dad equally loosely, "I expect you haven't taken much notice lately whilst understandably preoccupied, but NATFE the lecturers' union have been on about the very thing of poor wage relationships of HE/FE staff to school teachers. So in fact those of a Principal Lecturer grade and Professors, such as myself who don't have a tie in to a commercial interest, are paid less than most head teachers. School is the area of education that the government are pushing of course, with the 'Superteacher' further boosted salaries and the 'Superheads' who also have the additional sweetener of Knighthoods. Yet we've got more wooden-tops than ever as the majority of first year course applicants. Mind, to be fair, and some gladly are realizing it, it is because they've developed into a style of teaching to the test, as it becomes more prescriptive against a background of target management – the outcome is leaving us with more foundation work, mainly around ways of thinking and doing. But something positive on yours, and Lewis' side of things is that the Government are actually getting concerned about present take up of 'A' levels – where the likes of media studies is chosen over main sciences.

Anyway, to get back on track with our discussion point. We really do need to be outside of this jurisdiction, and to go forward with it, then there is always your Grandma Audrey's connection with Banna bay in Eire - again farm buildings, some unused." "Yes," I recalled, "I remember her saying about that connection, somewhere just above the Dingle Peninsula she said." Dad continued, "Yes, right next to the Atlantic at Banna Strand, as part of Ballyheige Bay. Because she was next of kin in the surviving members of the O'Hara family and to the owner of the farm, she actually gets a rental from the fellow working the land now. Paid by his accounts firm through the bank in Euros. She got me involved because she had their Tax Authorities on to her, from a tie up they had made of declarations, and they wanted her to pay income tax as the listed owner/assumed resident. So, there you have one possibly similar type of setting elsewhere, and I am sure the same type of farm equipment repair skills are equally in demand." "Well," I said, "for that matter specialising in the instrument pods and the like, we could probably have the actual units themselves handled by a secure carrier. Then it would not matter where in the British Isles we were, or should I more correctly say, where Lewis was. He may be able to support it better too with serviced replacements on a board or 'Eurocard' basis, and of course he could if necessary still do some in-situ work, going back to England for a day or so, travelling over himself on one of the cheap flights. Yes! I'm sure he'll go for it.

I wonder if it would be best to get all of Lewis' present gear by secure carrier, even though the important bit can get around by itself. They won't be able to detect any origin or source once outside of what we could loosely term their 'tunnel point sensor net'. But of course they could detect its latitudinal travel through the area, once it moves to repeated circumnavigating, or what Lewis calls its 'perimetric travel mode'. You know one revolution being equivalent to twenty-four hours 'back combing' if we can say that tongue-in-cheek. Essentially it would have to be sent south of London's Blackwall latitude early in the programmed movement. More or less first of all before crossing what we might call, fashionably and militarily our 'Exclusion Zone'." Dad then responded, in an equally of the cuff speculative way, "Of course what are now the Southern Irish, haven't involved themselves as a nation in any of the international war theatres, that have progressively become less about the quality and number of fighting men, and more about the number and sophistication of weapons. Their last engagement with 'foreigners' was probably the O'Briens in the west versus the Normans, around the 12th century and they won, beating off their 'Norman Invasion'." I laughed and rounded off by saying, "Mind, that was good score for the Irish. Of course I think I know from what's already been explored, that not being on the same island will not really matter to the technique of having to round the whole of the earth, but still an interesting point."

After a quiet moment of reflection I said, "You know though dad, Lewis has to be the most practical person I have met." "Yes, I am certainly impressed," came a quiet confirmation, "and not that it detracts in anyway from you, as you are three years younger. Oh that sounds clumsy! What I am trying to say is that I see these years for you as this fairly crucial time of an accumulation of development, into what I hope will be your independent thinking mind. I hope that makes some sense. But needless to say that Lewis is a bright and genuine guy, stick with him and you could learn a lot in your chosen field!" I am sure he was being complementary in his round about way, so I thanked him, and this only served to spur him on a bit more. But it was something I did need to hear, "I know I referred to your relative youth just then Paul, but I do want to say that I in particular certainly should not treat you like a child, which I can see I have done lately. When I've witnessed how well you've related, very much maturely, to what could be a deadly serious situation, I don't have an excuse. I can only say that you were a schoolboy a matter of months ago and I simply hadn't adjusted."

"No need to say any more Dad," I said and to steer us away from the imagined emotional violins. I referred simply and finally to the shared experience of the day with, "I know we have concluded a few of our thoughts here without Lewis, and I expect we are both uncomfortable with that. But I hope we all agree to pledge, that it's right for us not to speak of this 'til nearer the return. Several months of our time should see the 'heat' off our backs." "Yes," was the reply as we arrived home still in the conversational sound cocoon of the car, "save for some continued activity of mine in looking up the residential prospects. You know your mother would like to live in Eire, not just because of her roots, but also because of the relatively easy going country life. We both desire to get out of the rat race and obligations to direct employment.

Also save for one carrying forward reminder for you: Your Grandad Jim was in Hiroshima during October 1946. There was a working train in from the port of Kure, where he arrived on the Amethyst, and saw the aftermath first hand. Over a year later, but it would have to be many months beyond the bomb, to be safe enough on leave from the ship for a casual visit whilst he was nearby." "Hey!" I thought aloud, "If he is recorded as he wanders past, it would be good for him to see." "If there is something," said dad, " we'll see what we can agree between us. For if it's just presenting him with a DVD disk, if you and Lewis can find a way to separate each screenful of the full 360 degree hex of images, we can always put forward that it is from Pathe News Service." "Well yes of course, they do that now as a home order service from the Internet, we got him his grandad's sword-dancing as caught in action – remember? More seriously though, we would have to be very careful about the very existence of loose recordings. Although such a gift for grandad is a nice thought," I replied and dad nodded saying, "We'd also have to hope that his memory of the event is not still so complete and crystal clear. Such that he is prepared to contest the presence of a cameraman filming as he walked past, for then he might want to make an issue of it."

With that we both laughed as we both moved to get out of the car and into the house, and I warmed to the fact that this was much more of a 'matey' thing than we had experienced together before. It was good to feel such a firm sense of mutual trust and support, in no small way due to our new and shared involvement – I looked forward to more.

# CHAPTER SEVEN:
## SUSPENSION IS A PLANNING OPPORTUNITY

We all went about our business with an ideal of not lifting our heads until that eventual Thursday '555', having had all distractions, or should I say more correctly 'interesting attractions' taken away. Lewis and I were getting on well with our first year studies, having caught up on Lab. reports. Assignments being calendar placed were something we could not cram, for there were new college rules covering the formality of hand in times and extended time permits. So many hurdles involved that it's easier just to do it in line with the call up time, and in fair judgment it certainly seems a successful system all round.

This suggestion of my idea of interesting attractions makes me want to give assurance that Lewis and I weren't too geeky and did respond normally enough to social opportunities with our contemporaries, when afforded. Although beyond our part taking in the usually well-attended events of 'Freshers' Week', with being elsewhere, Lewis and I hadn't up to now made much more than the necessary contact with course mates. This away period however did give us a welcome break in keeping us out of the danger of becoming Techno-monks. Speaking mainly for myself that is, for I know Lewis was well into the habit (pun intended). It served as the tonic that normalised us into making more of student life. We looked into clubs and societies, giving the SFSoc a miss in case we got drawn into something that might compromise us, but did join the Real Ale Society, as it was good for organized coach trips to nearby cities. Edinburgh and York were memorable enough to us as moderates, that is compared to extremists whose over-indulgence left them with little memory of events, more especially of return journey(s), which they spent out of it on the luggage racks. Further to these experiences, I will have fond memories of the end of semester Fancy Dress do, particularly some art or fashion students – unsure because they were well disguised as very authentic looking Star Wars Storm Troopers – making their true identity come down to the best of belief as they looked magnificent with their bright whiteness reflecting the building lights against the dark background as we queued outside.

We did party well with good mixed company during this period, and both of us did consciously avoid trying to find that 'significant other', from the girls that is, although attempting to arrive at a shortlist was maybe okay for now. To those now disappointed, or even those who would have wondered up to this point about my no doubt close relationship with Lewis, I may need to clarify that it is the Boldon Flats that we occupy which is quite the opposite to the terrain and temptations of Brokeback Mountain!

Our determination with the Combing Back Through Time project could not be spoiled by such temporary fun though, and this was reflected equally with our full immersion into our studies, as we made the most of our time in this two-sided way. All in all, this was quite purposeful and in line with our plans. In a way I suppose, it was a bit like I had imagined it would be if someone has a life long ambition to be an astronaut, and they get offered the opportunity of a shift lasting a number of months on a space station. Their first concerns aren't going to be the number of weekend nights out on the town they are going to miss. It seemed true to my experience that losing sight of objectives just doesn't happen when faced with a very special privilege to come.

For our second year Extended Project Report, which we had to notify with an outline plan in advance, Lewis and I had also managed to get agreement to pair up. The area of study allowed was reasonably broad within Applied Sciences (not exclusively Physics); it just needs to represent an explored example which has commercial usefulness. Lewis did not want to cover the most obvious of his interests here anyway, wanting to keep time exploration strictly extra curricula. However he had intended to collect information in his special and quite unique way to cover another area, which was that of Cold Fusion, its beliefs/ revelations. Starting with Martin Fleischman and the work around his announcement of 23rd March 1989, on through the Sonic Fusion work of Sev Putterman, and into the believed success of Rusi Taleyarkhan. All of this, fortunately, is quite well documented currently, and it lends itself to direct evaluation as more present day active research. It means though that in being 'paired', the end result has to show twice the effort. We thought it was worth it in that showing successful co-operation would stand us in good stead for the next request, which would be to do our placement together as planned.

Dad was also into his bit and in his home time with mum was looking into the move. So much so they were going to take a long summer holiday over in Ireland to see the 'lay of the land' – they'd found a useful caravan site nearby to the farm in Eire at Ballyheige, further up on the bay, but still a short walk to the seafront. As we got further into summer, one evening with an intended session in the study, I came home to see the maps out on the kitchen table, with mum and dad stooped over them, with pans boiling in the background. "Not be long in cooking love," said mum as she moved to get on, "we are just getting quite excited over this," as she indicated with a slight twist of neck and a nod of head towards the table, both arms holding pans by this time. "Anyway get a quick wash and come straight back down, and you Jean-Paul we need the table now please!" Dad, in a very agreeable mood, stood up and while keeping the maps open, carried them over to a vacant bench shouting up after me, "Something here of interest to you son!"

We readily talked over the meal and by all accounts things were going well as dad had secured his agreed early retirement date of 20/06/05.

He also said that he would be able to chop at least about six weeks off by adding in his holiday entitlement, but he could decide that at the last minute, where it may be an alternative to leave on the day with a boosted pay packet. Should come in handy for incidental moving and travelling expenses, he would be thinking and one thing I certainly could not take away from him was preparation and contingency planning. Maybe something I'll learn more myself with age as it bothers me more. I just need to make sure that my placement pays sufficient to give me enough for the necessary local accommodation back here again, which reminded me:

"Dad, that reminds me, and this concerns you too mum," I said, with my dad looking a bit nervous, as I carefully skirted around things by continuing, "you know mum, how we were saying that in about a year's time, I'd be wanting to bring my friend Lewis over with me. Well I know its early yet, but we've being thinking of a tit-for-tat arrangement, where he stays with us for the placement months and in return I would have a room at his parents farm, down here on the Flats for the final study months. If we can work something out with our respective parents, which includes you! Then both of us will gain certainly as students with a minimal sacrifice from you." "It's food for thought Paul," mum said with dad nodding to show she spoke for both of them, "we'll bear it in mind – certainly good for you but it'll cost us something, and don't forget," she laughed, "dad will be a poor old pensioner, we'll have to 'cut the cloth'." Looking straight in to dad's eyes I then for now simply expected that he could read my thoughts, and that it was up to him to find his moment, to convince mum of some net side benefit from it.

"Well," dad said on reflection, "of course I will be well under sixty-five and if the history writing does not work out as an earner, that is once we've laboured a bit on getting the farm buildings more habitable. I could always tout my wares around the local colleges, or adult evening classes and the like." "Good to have contingencies!" I quoted back at him, something he always said. Then in mum's presence still for now, I had to keep to my own privacy of thought. It occurred to me though in all fairness, that if dad is set to make money from his writings and those writings have quite a unique contribution from Lewis' work, then there should be a contribution going Lewis' way. I am sure dad will think this when the time comes but I may still broach him with it later – having Lewis as an investigative contractor (a P.I.) – cool!

Following fairly easy first year success for both of us, thanks to being put to task during the more vital months of the course, Lewis and I were both keen to get away a bit as well as getting some earnings. So following up an advert for the sake of a change, on the Uni notice board, we had signed up as helpers at Butlins holiday camp in Wales, then to avoid the child care and chalet maid stuff, we'd told them that we were experienced bar staff. To bring that into line with reality, we took our first couple of weeks doing that very thing elsewhere, at the Caledonian hotel in Oban where we got in as summer seasonal student workers. With a little bit of planning ahead, we got a cheap one-way train fare each and there was accommodation with the job. We had a good laugh, enjoying our time with a South African guy and a couple of Canadians, we thought there must have been some international student advert out or similar, as it seemed temporary foreigners were there regularly.

We then came down the West Coast with our backpacks, staying at Youth Hostels, a couple in the Lake District, then in North Wales. Taking a week to get out to the holiday camp on the Welsh coast. Staying there only about a month we were keen to go, after exposure to all those 'wannabes' with their stage-struck antics. Keen to follow the likes of Des O'Connor from Redcoat to fur-coat so to speak, or worse – become stage struck politicians – 'they are the real stars' as Clint Eastwood said embarking upon his election campaign to be Mayor of his town of Carmel. Of course actors are true limelighters, whereas others see politics as another means of 'hogging the stage', and as long as there is a demand for 'talkers and not doers', attention seekers will stay on up there.

Back to our trip, and as planned, this last move took us pretty close to Swansea and a single ferry journey right around to Cork on Eire's southern east coast, a day or so from mum and dad and their last week in their six berth caravan. So it was after a ride on a horse drawn farm cart from just outside of Cork up the N22 that we arrived in Tralee, the nearest main town to the bay. The journey may have seemed quite Gypsy-ish, but these horse drawn vehicles are not at all unusual in Eire, as in fact the main trunk roads are quite accommodating, with dedicated slow vehicle lanes full length. Dad picked us up from there and we had a quick tour of the place in the summer evening light. It confidently felt a good idea for us all to have got to see the prospective new base, and indeed it did not disappoint. Importantly Lewis thought well of it.

Next morning both of us got stuck in to helping dad in particular with some of his physical tasks, in order to get them done in good time. By the end of the week we had actually managed not only to weather proof the farmhouse as accommodation, but also the main out building – important to Lewis and the plan. As the water was also now on, we resolved to come back at the mid autumn break to get the electricity on and set up a heating system of storage radiators which was simplest and seemed to be safer to be left for a while. Gas on this site was only portable and that was reserved for cooking preference. All in all the intention was to dry the buildings further through after the wet weather Banna had had lately and give us a chance to work here again at the Christmas break, into the night with lights.

So with this stage of work done and everything going to plan, we all left in dad's car, going north and over with the Stranraer ferry this time. A nice trip and we made a point of taking in some things for the first time, such as the 'Giant's Causeway'. Dodging down the back lane instead of using what he viewed as the extortionately priced car park. I could only think that this was an example of 'cutting the cloth' preparing for retirement, as dad was usually quite free with the cash on holidays. As usual mum's preparation included 'door-step' sandwiches, which added to the experience of a much more luxurious return journey for Lewis and I.

Christmas came and went and we were well into our second year with studies going well too. An Easter break spent over at Banna was just me and dad this time, with mum at home setting up a house sale and Lewis having to honour local repair work commitments as well as taking the opportunity on his rounds to prepare them for his absence from the summer. But we were well on and we had painting done, just for now in the ubiquitous magnolia. We then just waited for carpets before leaving, meaning next time it would be straight over and in with furniture. Chatting as we were painting, "Mum's certainly looking forward to a new life here," I said. "Yes, though she's got some old friends to leave behind," dad replied, "but as I've said to her, I'll be around all day (for better or worse). For that matter we'll all be around all day at first. Then if she still misses her own friends' company, she can invite them over for a stay, the ferries and flights are good and cheap enough." "Yes," I said in turn, "as long as we know about it we can plan around it. Though it maybe difficult if any wizz-bang-wollop from experimental work is being questioned." "I suppose we'll just have to believe that the lay person wouldn't suspect that equipment here would be anything other than agricultural engineering – for it would take an unlikely leap of their imagination, to consider time travel," dad reflected. "Of course that being said," I replied, "we still don't want anyone reporting, or even talking about anything they don't understand as notable or worse, 'suspicious things'." "Indeed," confirmed dad. "Oh yes!" I interjected, "that reminds me. Talking of notable things in the locality, the guy down the shop told me that the beach out there was used for some of the filming of 'Ryan's Daughter'. As I know this was many years ago, it should make us think that nothing much happens here." "A good word of caution then," said dad, "and another thing your mum mentioned, as we're in recall mode - she suggested to avoid any difficulties with time over the house sale that we simply rent it out. A lot of the gear is made to measure and won't fit readily into these old room shapes and sizes as well as the problem of transporting. Then of course it's always another base, we can always leave a live-in amount of stuff there, and the rental meantime will just about take up your mother's separate tax allowance as an income in her name." In unison we said, "Contingency," with some joy to end this trip.

# CHAPTER EIGHT:
RECOVERY

Time does fly when you are fully occupied, so before we knew it '555' was upon us. One possible advantage that we hadn't planned for, because it was announced more recently and well after Lewis set the date, and that was the Election. Something we thought might leave the national security interests, as a whole, with a major occupation away from any attention following up on our actions - although cautiously we might expect some.

When dad and I arrived, Lewis was in full attendance as we got to his still existing and re-activated workshop. "Should be any time now," he said. But a bit of gloom came to all of our faces slowly as the afternoon then night drew on with nothing to show. "Listen I need to go to a bit of a presentation tomorrow, to me that is, but I'll come here again afterwards," said dad, breaking the silence. "I'll stay here," I said, "we'll use those camp beds Lewis." He smiled at my gesture of support, so later that night, we tucked in adjacent to the bench in view of the show spot. "I like your dad, Paul. You can simply level with him, I think we'll get along fine," said Lewis. This made me pleased, not to say proud, for about the first time I can remember. Also happy in a new way that my dad was so intellectual, and certainly had been able to demonstrate the clear thinking side of his abilities. "He has certainly shown me more of the less obvious open minded side to his nature, if that's not a contradiction in terms?" I replied. We didn't need to say much more, although neither of us got much into deep-sleep as things were potentially dramatic close at hand.

Then suddenly at the crack of dawn Lewis jumped up saying that he had an idea and before I could respond, was in and out of the farmhouse with a metal detector. Then he spoke, "I've just said 'hi' to my dad in the house there, he's up very early getting his breakfast as he wants to get a good many hours on a job before midday sun today – gonna be a hot one on the forecast. You see this is a contrast in parents, yours to mine. I do love them both dearly, and they certainly let me alone where most students would think that the opposite of that was an essential reason not to live and study at home. It's only sometimes in the past I've wished they would take some interest in what I am doing." "I understand," I found myself saying in genuine appreciation, "not being able to share such a brilliant what do we say? Discovery/invention/development, it must eat you up." "Well," he concluded, "it may be for the best at the moment that mum doesn't just wander in to say 'tea's ready' and prefers the local intercom I set-up. Of course dad's mainly out in the fields and from dawn – a very traditional farmer him. Then at night he just disappears behind the local evening paper before he's off to bed early." Then I rounded with, "And like me you're an only one. That's probably for the best as well, as far as undisturbed use of 'these toys' goes." With that and a smile, Lewis swept the detector plate over the area to an accompanying beep-beep, continuous at the centre-point of the 'landing strip', for want of a better word for a dedicated area on the concreted floor. "That's what I thought," he said, "it's under here," pointing at the concrete floor. "Then I can't just get the pneumatic drill on the job with my old man still within earshot – I'll have to think!"

After a few minutes of deliberation, Lewis spoke up again, "I know, I'll tell him that I've had a problem with subsidence and floor cracks due to moles." "How big are the moles?" I humoured. "No it's not that tall a story," replied Lewis, "you see the confirmation I needed came from the detector, but the tell tale sign was the rippling of the track at the back of the barn here, producing lumps of fresh earth. We'd find it equivalent in volume to a one-metre sphere. You see if it had returned say to the left of where it was, then the spatial fold would just shift across – think of it more like a 'sausage balloon' with a squeeze of air moving a shape from one end to the other. Appearing underground however, means more than that simplest case of air displacement as it reforms, because it then needs to displace its volume in soil. So here it has pushed it out at the first point of least resistance in the direction of travel. That is, just past the concrete raft of the barn. In all cases though the universal spatial forces are re-balanced with it appearing actual shape and size in today's time and space 'slot' if you like, where it belongs."

Later when my dad came back in to the building, Lewis had already been out to chat to his, and followed in saying, "Well I've got the okay to start digging!" My dad (Prof) then looked around in surprise, to which Lewis went on to explain, "Yes, the reason why we can't see it is that it is a good few feet under the floor! It will be sitting on sea level which is a hard-wired default setting for when digital control has a problem relocating it. It's actually a good reason why your new place is also low lying and flat. In fact it maybe worth laying the floor at sea level in any case, that is if it is practical within the new work shed. Just a thought – anyway my dad thinks I am just re-levelling this one and first it needs digging out." "What did he say about that?" I asked. "Oh just that he did not have time to help," replied Lewis, "and that I should get 'me mates' on to it – that's you guys – so its all above board and he has no reason to come in here."

Dad (Prof) then said, "Hold the bus a moment, this may actually be handy the way it is. For when I was at the gathering 'in my honour' this morning I made a point of talking to a Solid State Physics lecturer, Ben Rudden, you know him," as we nodded. "Yes well he's a bit further up the tree than when he interviewed you as course tutor two years ago. Suffice to say, I was able to ask him knowingly if there had been any word from DDA/Nat. Phys, and he said, 'funny you should say that, but we have just had a call this morning asking if we were doing any project work in association with the technology units on Boldon

Business Park'." "Round the corner from here!" I said in confirmation of what all three of us were thinking, "They've obviously got their new detector array on to yesterday's movements, and you mean leaving it out of sight and not disturbing it would be best until they've safely gone." "Yes," confirmed dad, looking at us both with Lewis nodding in agreement, "if it was here to be seen I was going to suggest putting in the hired van. We've got it from this weekend to take a few things over that we don't want to leave to the furniture van guys." "Take the benches and larger equipment then, I'll just need some essentials to use. I know that I won't be able to down load after recovery here, but there's plenty of time to come," suggested Lewis.

Next morning back home, it was Saturday and dad rose pretty casually more specially as he and mum had been invited out for a celebratory retirement meal. As it was optional for me I gave it a miss. "Enjoy last night then," I said as I poured him out a coffee from a pot I had already brewed. "Yes," he replied, "we just went to a gastro-pub rather than an Indian or Chinese, mainly for us both to keep our digestion sound for the next few days of packing and travelling. It gets you like that when you get to our age. Anyway, I've got a bit of good news for both you and Lewis, so if you can, go and get him and offer him the chauffeur treatment back up here, 'elevenses' plus some useful info to share."

With that I went down to the farm and as I drove into the gateway, I pulled up next to Lewis' mother who was outside the farmhouse door. "Good morning Mrs. Taylor!" I shouted over. "Hello Paul," she replied, "I suppose your coming to see Lewis," (I nodded). "Well he's in the shed as you might expect, I'll go in here and buzz him to let him know before you get in there." I did just that and things in his 'inner sanctum' looked pretty bare. "Hi Paul," he said, "I am just wrapping up here as we'll be taking advantage of Prof.'s offer to transport the instrumentation etc. Also when I break up the concrete here it'll be best to have things out of the way of all the dust." "Good!" I replied, "and talking of my dad

(Prof) he would like me to bring you back with me, he has something to say to both of us." "Yeah sure!" Lewis agreed, "I could do with some time out as I am just about finished here for now."

Back at our house in the study, dad started by saying, "I firstly want you to be assured Lewis, that this is news to both of you and this is an example of how we should all treat anything vital. You see I certainly don't want you to get any impression or concerns that because Paul and I have the obvious connection, anything of significance would be revealed without your knowledge or involvement." "Yes," confirmed Lewis, "that's welcome, and I believe we can take that to operate three ways." "The only way!" I added. "Anyway," dad continued, "this is something to relax us, and I don't mean the coffee, although you scientific types will probably correct me telling me that it is a stimulant (smiling). To get to the point though last night at my 'retirement treat' I spoke to an old friend, Colin Snape, who actually used to be a Geophysics specialist from your department at college, but left to take up a senior post in charge of all field operations at N.E.D.L. - the electricity distribution people." "Mind he was teaching us electrical stuff," I added. "Well that's not unusual for undergrad lecturing," affirmed dad, "I am sure he'd be apt with both as it is also quite relevant to his new job. Anyway, he was from a farming family just like yourself Lewis, experience which came in handy for 'field' operations you might say, but funnier than that, in his interview he actually said that as a geophysicist he knows how the land lies. Success followed and he's one of their main men now, covering Y.E.D.L. (Yorkshire) as well with countless staff and expensive access equipment within his budget. Some weird experimental all terrain vehicles that I am sure would interest you." Lewis saw this as an invitation to ask, "Who does his repairs?" "Oh, I am sure it is just contracted in with the supplier, just like fire engines by lease agreement," dad replied.

He continued to smile when I felt I should prompt him, "Come on dad, we've got Lewis here especially to hear what you have to say." "Yes of course," rounded dad, "I am sorry to go on, but the only reason for being light right now is because I think we can all lighten up. You see Colin had a visit from the National Physical Lab, accompanied by the DDA and the Transport Police, wanting details of any unusual power surges in the Boldon Area on the 5th May. An incidental thing he let out when I was trying to sell him the benefit of early retirement, by asking him about the most interesting thing that had happened to him today. Also I am sure he wasn't breaking any confidences with that – no customer information there."

"Well," said Lewis carrying some humour from the earlier moment, "firstly it's interesting to see the transport police trying to get onto the ground floor of time travel developments. But having said that, it does show us that they don't know what they are looking for at all. At this stage at most they can only be looking for what they may suspect as a synthetically, or for that matter accidentally, generated time-slip which they are presuming consumes a lot of power - having some sort of fixed plant. They have no idea that we have been using a self powered or self contained device." "Fixed versus portable! That's more or less what I believed was the significance, Lewis," replied dad, "and thank you for stating it so comprehensively." Lewis smiled then said, "So with that as a relief, I'll get straight back and break up the concrete this afternoon. Making a noise during acceptable hours, and if you guys could help me with a bit of the spade work later, after dark would be best, we'll sort it all before the weekend's out."

We agreed, and did just that. Three of us made short work of the digging and dad making conversation said, "I was thinking, maybe incorrectly you'll be telling me, that there's some interesting things in the history of right here. From Bede to the recent sea-arch collapse. The story of the Boldon Book, the North East equivalent to the Doomsday Book." "Yes," I jumped in, "and the item I was interested in as you'll recall dad, the alleged 'boat of Scandinavian origin', supposedly in the upper reaches of the river Don. Just a small tributary now, but in the days of Canon Savage who observed it, it was much larger before they completed digging the irrigation channels across the Flats. However, the only trouble with both of these is precise dates and places." "That is certainly something," answered Lewis, "though it can be segmented with a once a week image or whatever, or repeated visits with steps in between to make its absence from base shorter. That is shorter in our real time waiting experience. But the point I think Prof is making leads me to clarify that being here now, is no advantage in getting back to here earlier in time. Because of course there is one full perimetric journey per day back over, whether it's here or somewhere else. Either way doing it here or doing it from the new site at Banna, will both involve movement through the Sensor Net with the coverage including this area."

Shortly and pertinently as a lull developed, we got to the shiny top with the pattern, which was now familiar to us. Then we gave the old man a breather and just Lewis and I continued. There was only really room in the hole for two of us and by then we had to use hand trowels and a hearth brush, so as not to add to any damage. Making a recovery from the hole was easier than I expected. It wasn't particularly heavy and we used a sling-set hung over the rafters which Lewis told us was used for getting beasts onto their feet. Or even holding horses up with a leg or hip injury to take the weight off, they might even sleep in the sling in a standing position until they heal.

With that little bit of imparted farming knowledge we paused, to let Lewis do a brief examination, as he opened the panel. "Oh yes, tut-tut! Thought as much," he said, "there's been no explosive that is to say 'mechanical' affect from the bomb as you may see, but the terrific light intensity has overloaded the CCD." I looked across at dad's interested but puzzled face and contributed with, "Charge Coupling Device – it's the basis of all video images these days, but you can critically overload them just like our own eyes." "Yes," agreed Lewis, "the reason I thought it would be affected was the loss of ground level sensing. You see it uses the CCD when over the open sea, which on average it is more than it is on land, where the image processing looks to minimising the earth's curvature. So with the camera below the waistline it maintains a reference with sea level '0'. It doesn't matter what it 'ploughs' through in the way of combing space, inclusive of solids etc. round the shell. But when it comes to a stop it has to have a reference to solid surfaces. It should also default as it begins to stop, to position itself above densities greater than its own. This is of no matter when it's travelling, you could almost see that as being in an extremely low orbit, but it does mean though that it will not stop and float on water. Whilst there is a deliberate reasoning here to do with stability, it has further limitations with say observing meetings in multi-floor buildings (our naturally occupied 'air-gaps' between floors). I've still got to get round that adequately." Lewis then added as he looked down, "And this outcome means that there'll be nothing recorded from the blast onwards, there or subsequently!"

"I am thinking whilst you're talking Lewis," I said. "Something I can't quite grasp is - if the CCD was affected by high intensity Electro-magnetic Radiation, and we know that the visible spectrum of this EmR is transmitted through to the recorder, then the very transmission of such energy would do damage to all circuitry surely? I mean this is the problem that the military were always worried about in the event of a nuclear blast, with computerised weaponry and battlefield telecomms etc." "Good issue to raise," replied Lewis, "but it hasn't, and I only reason out for now that the blast was 'above', if we can say that when talking interspace, where it would effectively be presented by a further condensed point, at the polar spike, to that source of all produced wavelengths of EmR. There is though a reflective silver panel set presented at most of the surfaces, meeting this radiation, with the exception of the camera panel being to the underside. A 'whiting out' of the CCD only was maybe because of it principally being reflected radiation, other wavelengths acting a bit differently taken through to the interspace with different intensity. I am thinking of absorption versus reflection from the ground and/or surroundings, and just what wavelengths are maintained, though I confess that can only be conjecture. We would only really understand it by 'scientific method and experimental design' but I wouldn't want to go again. After all who knows, we may have been just 'lucky'? But it's an opportunity for a newer more up to date replacement CCD now, one with better low light 'lux' levels, dynamic range and higher resolution. It might have helped more with the Kennedy images if I had upgraded earlier, but then it has only been breakdowns where I've allowed for new parts. Not having the luxury of the relatively high budget of 'official' research."

Lewis' explanation of level referencing raised a question in dad's mind, and so after he'd patiently listened, he asked, "What about the Spanish Armada, or other great events at sea?" "To witness them," answered Lewis, "we'd have to locate onto the deck of a ship." I then made my contribution, "I had thought that whilst we have this infinitely thin occupied space, that the density of the probe would be unaffected." "Yes that's true," confirmed Lewis, "it doesn't act with infinite pressure akin to a 'needle point' on the floor, as the floor immediately beneath it is of the same respective density. We need to imagine it as affecting an extended column into other material, flaring out from the base, as the warping influence dissipates. At the polar spike though, the field tends to follow it more as a point."

Dad then stepped in with, "I may even be surprising myself to say that I am still with what you are describing, maybe I can better fathom it through today. It strikes me though that we need to be sure of what we are doing right now, are you wanting to put this in the hire van? That is to go with Tish and I in a couple of day's time, Monday or maybe Tuesday the way things are going? Or as Paul is bringing the car over with our cat, and other incidental items which don't take up a lot of space, in what is a Land Rover Discovery, you can easily fit it into what is more than a metre square of load space, when carrying just two people?" "Yeah – good Prof thanks," answered Lewis, "we'll go for that second option."

# CHAPTER NINE:
## SETTING UP AGAIN

So next thing, with dad well under way a day or so ahead, Lewis and I arrived at Stranraer, or more precisely Cairnryan further up the loch, for a fast ferry trip to Larne in Northern Island. Fortunately items in the back were mainly showing through as a heap of domestic removals. That, together with the processing of the cat in his holding basket and the detailed examination of his vaccination certificates, took away any further search enthusiasm at the docks. Then we were simply underway, followed by a lengthy drive down to Banna, on Irish 'N' roads. These are allegedly equivalent to our 'A' roads, with the proviso that you need the robust suspension of something like a 4x4 to survive them. It's the sudden change of road style, with the yellow dotted marker line for the dedicated inside slow lane, together with the immediate undulations, that is how you'd know that you've crossed the border.

Lewis had been the first to actually raise an important, late yet unresolved issue while we travelled on, when he asked about mum's involvement, whereas dad and I had just knowingly dodged around it. "Your mum (Tish) is going to be the fourth person close at hand here, with some unavoidable involvement you know, and I have been long resigned to the fact that we would probably have to take her into our confidence. It's a bit different to my mum and dad being out of it quite willingly, just getting on with their own thing, after all your mum is married to one of our number – your dad." "Well knowing dad," I replied, "if he hasn't said, he certainly won't have told her. He's always had a knack of compartmentalising in that way. We'll check it out with him as soon as we can see him on his own – tomorrow." Later that night we arrived and were nonetheless enthusiastic about a new dawn to a new day, and a new hopefully undisturbed life plan full of our intentions.

Next morning even though we had had a tiring journey we somehow felt more 'live-wire' than expected and soon joined dad with mugs of coffee in hand, out by what was a boundary fence post. "Nice air here," he said once we got over to him. Straight away I mentioned what was on our minds, "Yes it is, and I am glad the three of us are here and out of earshot right now, for Lewis and I were talking on the way here about the extent of mum's involvement." "Well certainly she's here at the site of this project," replied dad, "and I can see us tripping ourselves up unless she has some awareness. That is, enough to settle her mind over all of us and our activities, but not necessarily as far as 'involvement'," and seeing the obvious relief and affirmation in our faces, dad went on. "I'll tell you something about Tish, Lewis, at the risk of covering ground familiar to Paul, but then I've known her for even longer than he has (snigger). She is a very intelligent woman and her talents lie principally in the Arts. Though in many ways, she can also be more practically inclined than I am when the mood takes her. She came from an Operatic family…." I interrupted, "- And you always told me, when I was younger that you encouraged her to run away with you from a Circus". "Yes, well it was like a bit of a circus in their house, they certainly had a menagerie of animals," was dad's response. "I suppose it's better than saying she ran away from a Zoo!" I chuckled, "I just imagine the teasing if I had told my school mates that." "Steady now! That's the light of my life we're talking about," said dad in a pseudo-serious voice. We all smiled and he continued, "Tish is more inclined to fiddle with the technical side of computers and the like than I am. Also talking about fiddling, she is an accomplished musician capable with the violin and other guitar like items, whether four course or six course (strings to the uninitiated). She's got the lot as well as a keyboard controller with a programmable sound generator/tapeless recorder thing. She can also sing with an Operatic voice that her parents were able to be proud of, and she can only improve with age on that if she continues to practice. Could've even made a career with it, which we considered seriously before Paul was born." "Why didn't you?" Lewis asked. "It was the pressure of expectation to do the 'normal' thing," replied dad, "I had a Research Assistantship at the University with a promise of good career development and I would have to drop it to travel around - me carrying her music I suppose. Oh, and she can also paint and sculpt. She did this and History of Art at Uni and that's where we met.

So with relevance to our activities here, I am sure she'd like nothing better than the opportunity to watch the great painters paint. But what I really would like to see her do is fulfil her second ambition with horticulture. She's developed a keen interest in the beauty of flowers and she's well into the genetic selection and breeding side. Nothing better than to achieve a new variety that she can name. A satisfying step into immortality don't you think? Anyway, she does know that Lewis is with us to work in that allotted building (pointing) with you Paul, and is interested about some of your work, which I did make her aware of, and in particular Lewis - market gardening automation equipment. This may be the extent to which she may wish to get involved. She also knows, of course, that I am now going into full-time writing about historical events and some new interpretations, but she does not know your connection with it, or should I say more importantly, 'the unique facility being afforded to this work'. Apart from that I know Tish can be trusted." "That goes for me too Lewis," I added, "without question!" "Okay then Prof," said Lewis, "maybe we'll just see how it goes along, and if Tish shows a greater growing interest and asks involved questions, then we'll answer them. More of a 'leave it out and don't mention it' rather than 'intended deception' then – agreed?" We all nodded.

"Right then dad," I made a further take up on the occasion for raising points, "as to the connection with your writing and prospective publishing. You should really contract with Lewis, by gentlemen's agreement if you like, some sort of royalty payment for the research/use of tools, or whatever." "Yes indeed," he replied, "there are agreed rates for contracted researchers, we'll work something out around that." "Thanks Prof." Lewis replied. "Pleasure," said dad, "indeed I expect it will be a pleasure, as well as a unique privileged involvement for all three of us."

He said more, "And now that we continue to keep all things above board, I'll reveal something further to you both – my dream last night: I thought that the place name 'Banna' had been picked up by the interested authorities (D.D.A), and I felt pleased that I had successfully way-laid them to Birdoswald, just off the road to Carlisle. That's because it was an ancient Roman fort called 'Banna'." Lewis' good knowledge of the history of science and technology came in again when he asked, "Isn't that somewhere near the old 'Blue Streak' rocket testing site at Spadeadam?" Dad nodded and smiled, and I then said, "Well, maybe we can create a misleading trace there." "Certainly it's possible," confirmed Lewis confidently, "we'll keep it in mind as a contingency." "See dad!" I exclaimed, "All three of us talk the same language now." With that dad laughed, and I could see our pact was working as we were all in good spirits.

From there we moved back towards the door with empty mugs swinging in hand, meeting my mother shouting in a light hearted voice, "Don't throw those around lads! We've only got half a dozen, because I have had to leave enough items for use in our 'furnished' let in Boldon."

# CHAPTER TEN:
## RETRIALS IN EARNEST –
## BACK IN ACTION

That afternoon, mum left us for town to have a look around and familiarise herself with facilities, provisions etc. and this gave us a direct opportunity to meet round the table. Lewis started speaking, "Well folks! As you may recall, I wanted to look at levelling the useable floor area of the New Lab here down to sea level, and this is in the light of our last experience. But as we're wanting to push forward it can wait." I then asked, "With care when operating round the directly vacant space, could it possibly be done while 'on mission' so to speak?" "Yes," Lewis confirmed, "we can handle that, and as to the initial setting up, whilst I am confident of it, help is appreciated as it will get us away earlier - 'many hands make light work'."

Lewis went on to say, "We should agree a 'Mission List', with a bias of course on Prof's essential work." "I know that I have been thinking out my preferences," said dad, "I am sure we can knock up a first draft right now." "Yes," agreed Lewis, "make it about a dozen – times with locations" "What about a bakers' dozen?" I said, "Let's fly in the face of unlucky numbers, I am sure we are all beyond superstition. I'll start out with a follow up on Kennedy – 'Who killed Marilyn?'" "Well," replied dad, "that takes us straight away into moral aspects of this. It would be quite voyeuristic to just record events in her boudoir prior to the believed time of her death." "Not only that, we have a technical problem of hotel multiple floors, as I mentioned before. Something which I will work on, but today I don't have a solution to that as an enhancement," said Lewis. "Okay, but we still do need to install some ground rules and boundaries as a matter of Project Policy," continued dad, "I for example would like to know what happened to the Nazi bullion, the legendary hidden treasure. But there is a moral issue, what could we rightly do with the knowledge? It's not right to go and get it and somehow spend it, and not right for many other interested parties to find out either. I mean if we happen to image something it can't be helped, and we can only censor videos at best, for example I expect there will be abhorrent scenes of any massacre. Then there's the religious world, for example, witnessing the Resurrection. If there was actual knowledge, which we may obtain, that would then be known as 'the truth' or something beyond faith, where faith is itself the core of religion, then that can only lead to mass social disruption. After all, there is enough trouble as it is, not only between faiths but between the next level down of interpretations of the same faith, and that's without any period evidence video material coming into it."

"Can I just say as well," added Lewis, "just to be sure we understand, we don't need to stay away from something like the 'Hundred Years War'. Because of segmented recording it doesn't disqualify it. So it's not as if we need to necessarily wait around for a hundred years." "As it happens, I thought we'd just want to select a couple of key events in such as that," acknowledged dad. "Good then," said Lewis with a smile, "and we should always remember the forethought, that the better likelihood of fruitful results comes from the better reliability we have of time and place. Also, we must keep in mind two known technical problems, with multiple floors as per design limitation today, and high light intensity as per experience – I don't want to blow the new CCD on its first outing."

We further talked over our thoughts and came to an agreed listing of thirteen. Lewis wanted unfinished business covered, not risking Hiroshima again, but to get to the bottom of the Man on the Moon question with N.A.S.A. He could not wait or be sure of how conclusive the Japanese high-res orbital camera shots would be, or for that matter how we may have them reported to us in the West. I do sense that in fact behind all three of us is a motivational desire to not only 'know' what we are 'told'.

Dad's list as expected was structured, as he was doing his first book on Churchill, and the principal decisions leading to turning points in the Second World War determination and moods amongst all who were involved, significant changes of mind or direction. As a result there are quite a chain of visits close on time and place. Lewis and dad also thought it would be a good trial just to see how far one can go with visual interpretation, without sound for quite an intense subject, to grasp fully all limitations for dad's type of need. I suppose we can always hope that a lip-reading software package will be available soon, which we believe should be a development on Intel's 2003 AVSR open sourced firmware and, if audio output is too much to expect, I am sure just sub-titling would be a welcome aid. They pretty much up to live translation to text on TV now, of course that is from an audio source and sound pattern, rather than video with what would be here a type of purely visual source of movement.

On the day of this listing though, I could only think quickly of Cleopatra and the asp, whether this was actually true. Something there had been a TV programme about recently. Also I wanted it to impress with this being perhaps more academic than my interest in Marilyn – a beauty still though by all accounts. Dad reluctantly wrote it down, saying he couldn't at first think it was very different to the point he made about Marilyn, but then also said he must make allowances, as he could just about remember what it was like to have the hormones of youth. "Mind if beautiful women is your subject," he added, "there's supposedly none more so than Helen of Troy, and then usefully you could confirm the growing legend, amongst Afro-American academics, that she was black."

"Okay then, what about the incident of Harold getting shot in the eye?" I suggested as my alternative. Dad wrote that also with some reluctance, with a slight twist to his mouth, saying further, "The place is quite away in land from Hastings and today is called 'Battle', and I suppose to work this out you'll have to select a good open view (pausing). I need to tell you more of what I mean. The proceedings were that Harold's men were set up in a full mile long line with locked shields on the high ridge. It is only when efforts to break them up were eventually followed, just before twilight hours, by the Duke of Normandy's instructions to his bowmen to use an irregularly high trajectory that one in the rain of arrows struck Harold. So because of this you'd have to be pretty much on the line of shields, on the ridge itself, to view both sides unobstructed." I then brought up a query directed at Lewis, "I am not sure I know how this one, and London as dad is thinking, fits with our intention to observe a restriction over the U.K. mainland. Another thought then is, surely if it's worth going to 60 degrees South to commence the perimetric stage, on any trip back, then it's going to be worth it on this one for around a thousand years." "Yes Lewis do we take it that we can avoid a crossover?" Asked dad. "Oh, it's straight forward really," replied Lewis confidently, "it drops 'down', if we can say that, as a spiral path and then returns in over the south coast, to Hastings in this case." "Missing the detector net altogether!" I added, and then we all went silent for a moment to mull over the situation.

"Right then," said Lewis, "we do need to re-trial it. We can probably bundle a number of the World War II views together sequentially, which I'll have to plan out, and we probably need to talk further Prof about what you might be hoping for in relation to what I have seen as possible. By that I mean when we are trying to follow up on people and places quite so intensely we still have the ground level limitation, so a site underground at the Whitehall Buildings, where you say Churchill had his War Cabinet, could be a problem in another way. As well as what I've said of course, we are only able to visually record and deduce all verbal contributions, lip-reading skills have to be our own for now." "That means Hitler and his bunker's out dad!" I quipped. "Well," he replied with a smile and his usual sharp wit, "should that be the case, I'll just have to settle myself with that hotel in South America where he's supposed to have stayed after the War. If we can see him go in or out of the front door, then he wasn't killed in the bunker." "By the way," as I recalled from what was just mentioned, "I read something about lip-reading you know. We all lip-read in association with our normal auditory perception. A guy called McGurk did experiments to show, for example, that if the word 'park' is said over and over to someone not looking, and if someone then mouths the word 'dark' over it, with a clear 'd' mouth shape, then the subject starts to hear 'dark' because of this paired perception. Called the 'McGurk Effect' – just thought it would be a point of interest."

"I think for trials, best to do yours first Paul," prompted Lewis, "'Battle of Hastings' I mean your second choice. A fairly precise time and place out of doors." "- And it'll cut the remaining list down to twelve from unlucky thirteen!" I quipped. "Who's counting?" Lewis then said with a newly expressed technique of throwing his voice out of the side of his mouth like a ventriloquist. With that we all laughed as Lewis folded the list handed over by dad, and put it in a wallet for safe keeping, also saying as he did, "That's not all the writing either, I intend formal lab type reporting, one report per trip." "Good discipline!" dad exclaimed, and again we had a round of nods in agreement.

Later that week we picked another home alone period for the 'green-light' to go to 'Battle' on Saturday 14th October 1066. With a full recharge, and after Lewis checked out the recording and playback to his satisfaction, we were treated to another fascinating visual display. Albeit as seen through shaded safety goggles and this first new mission was off without a hitch. "Something else," Lewis spoke to clarify, "though not applicable to the trial just set away, I do need to go over segmented recording with you both. It can be done whilst staying on the spot which is simply via the recording time program, with energy being saved at dormant times – just like what I set up for the Hiroshima site. But in the example mentioned earlier of the 'Hundred Years War', it would not be practical for us to wait for one hundred years with or without a form of periodic recording. In such a case it would have to be segmented travel, through the travel program, where we would get back a segmented recording without having the real time wait. You can really say that 'life's too short'." With some broad satisfaction that we all understood, we then could only wait, with the present recording mission being away for just under two days. This included a minimum sort of overlap to cover before-and-after events around the level of precision we were able to use.

Work on all round improvements can be made to the site still during missions, especially with present needs, in anticipation of some placement work coming in soon for Lewis' and my intended partnership whilst we are here. Of course dad will do a bit of this together with his writings, and I am sure we can all help mum too with her set up. A healthy outdoor farm life at least new to three of us!

As intended on the third day, after a faultless return, we were watching a recording on the hex screen system, taking turns in the chair. "This is good stuff for someone well into studying military thinking, past errors of strategy/positioning and all that," said dad, "but for us it's more of a 'who's who'." Sure enough Lewis was able to use digital zoom better than before with the latest CCD, and this did give us a clear image of King Harold. I remembered that before this, the only image in my mind was a copy embroidered section of the Bayeux Tapestry, on the wall in my Year Four at Primary school, with him leaning back holding an arrow shaft. Now there it actually was, on the screen 'in the flesh' so to speak.

We were able to frame-by-frame reverse video with the zoom, and trace the trajectory back to a bow held by a Norman. "That's him!" I exclaimed, as he was brought into somewhat grainier closer focus. "Yes, Paul, but who is he?" Responded dad, and he continued to exemplify, what he believed useful from an academic research point of view, "Whilst it is an amazing position to be in to be able to see such a thing (goriness accepted), we need to have something which makes a difference. As we could be no further forward in identifying the archer, and for that matter, identify him for what? Too late for wanted posters and punishment, and so altogether for that matter, quite 'pointless'." He finished with a less serious face, after a round of smiles at his choice of words, "We may as well just call him 'Norman'."

The lesson was learned!

# CHAPTER ELEVEN:
## WHAT DOES OUR FUTURE HOLD?

Next morning we gathered around the equipment bench, there was easily enough room for us three to sit around one edge on a newly installed set of bar stools, something which my parents managed to purloin in an afternoon's walk about, as surplus to the hotel's refitting up the road. I suppose you could see it as a 'before they hit the skip' episode rather than a favour to friends. Still, it means that my parents are mixing a bit with the indigenous folk and that's no bad thing.

Our intention was to have a debriefing, or a 'wash-up' meeting as may be seen in a non-militaristic, preferred way. Still formal enough to satisfy Lewis' need to install such a feature as a routine aspect to our operation. Dad was equally keen, and I could also accept the need for proper formal functioning. Whilst a danger of keeping notes is discovery, in that you can keep anything with you that you can carry in your head, we wanted to keep a lab report, completed with setting parameters as well as observations, for each mission – something agreed with Lewis earlier.

I spoke first, "I know you've got the settings down there Lewis including the timings, and that's good, but something which occurred to me for the first time this morning, as I came out to walk over here mulling over yesterday's events, was what about the actual travelling time? I mean that this should vary noticeably surely?" "Yes it does," Lewis sharply replied, "and for this last trip I did have to allow for that. Tens of years back, which is the range I've stayed in so far wasn't perceptibly different, but one thousand years back to 1066 was. As I say I allowed for it, but we still had it coming back same day more or less." "It must be about 'C' then I reckon," I asked with a half puzzled look, to which Lewis responded, "Yes, and this I expect will be a limiting factor to just how far back we can go." Dad was just sitting there attentively taking things in, when Lewis turned to him with immediate assurance saying, "It won't be anywhere near your range of dates of course, and as to the issue itself as a good point by Paul, it certainly seems true to logic that missions are unaffected by frictional or any mechanically resistant forces, and that would include inertia and momentum acting very differently – explaining the surprisingly very low power consumption in travelling.

So it is limited by the speed of the switching circuitry, also at 'C' (light speed) and it does have a pattern of incremental/discrete movement, rather than a continuous/smooth flow. Without these hindrances, it should have a ceiling value of 'C', the universal maximum, but at our best position of 60 degrees, I've measured that it achieves about ten revolutions per second, as experienced by the outside observer(s) – us!" "Just a moment now, I am with that," said Dad looking up at the ceiling, "counting that 10 days a second, that's 600 days a minute, and 36000 days an hour, or about one hundred years per hour." "That's what I like to hear Prof," said Lewis, "a quick bit of mental arithmetic, I am formerly from the workaday world and sometimes it's a lifesaver. I say that knowing that some of the younger school leavers would find that a bit alien as an experience, present company accepted." Meaning me, but then dad immediately countered with, "I wouldn't have him any other way, but sharp enough on sums, science course or not. As I think I may have said to you both before, I could see the way basic numerical agility was slipping within the student body – an increased use of calculators and handy laptops. I won't get started on writing skills and the phenomenon of the one page sentence," "Grammar checkers should help there though dad," I said to question his position on that last item. "Oh, some think that because the word processing packages are American English, they should ignore them – clues ignored by the clueless in some frustrating cases," he relayed, "and mind I'm listening out for the first department to consider phone text as an accepted medium for short answer assignments – making them shorter still!" This got a knowing silent smirk from Lewis and I. "Anyway if you see me as chairing this session, I must call us to order as we are drifting off here," remarked Lewis.

"Right, you have power management with a 'time-out' predicting circuit, I remember you saying Lewis?" I asked him to confirm. "Yes, and as we get increasing confidence with missions and have sufficient available waiting time we could actually confirm the maximum period of travel, as it will return at the point of having enough stored energy to reverse its movement." "I suppose it would be best not to go too far - anywhere near a proto-earth anyway," dad humoured. "Interestingly enough as well," Lewis added, "as it is unaffected by ground features, and doesn't rely on them for geographical positioning, then it is unaffected by plate-tectonic movement." "- And that can be something," I contributed, "in the longer periods at 2cm per year." "Yes, 'the rate your nails grow', I read somewhere," added dad, and something then to check out, in the near few thousand years, is the view first put forward by Hapgood that the Earth also has an overall loosely fitted 'skin' in the upper layer(s). Early map makers had Antarctica away from where it is now and without ice!"

"So as it is, what do you guesstimate for a maximum trip Lewis?" I asked curiously. "I can't put a number on it," he replied, "but I think 'dinosaur days' are out - for now anyway and even though energy is consumed in very short bursts once underway, I would still look to portable power improvements that can be made with better battery technology – but then some periods of prehistory are achievable, though it takes some waiting around for us here, as I've outlined." "Not back to early hominids for now then," I remarked. Dad then countered by saying, "That's not unless we explore legendary sightings of the so called 'wild man'. You know they are reputed to have lived around Southern England in the 13th Century, named as 'woodwoses' - maybe one for the next list?"

"Anyway," dad continued, "Lewis! I know we have drifted a bit from a formal meeting, in no small way due to me. Importantly though I believe I am gauging things correctly, when I say it seems that we are all happy with yesterday's performance." "Yeah, sure," said Lewis, "and I think that's a wrap for the meeting. A good bit of intelligent friendly banter is probably worth more to us at this stage." With this, we all looked around at each other with slight, but warm and knowing smiles, as an acknowledgement of the comfort we felt as a team. This can only take us forward in a cooperative way, and in turn can only help challenge any confidence issues that may arise with our hoped continued secrecy as intended for the foreseeable future.

Then a not wholly irrelevant coincidence as we are into 'Chapter Eleven', is that this term is used in the U.S. by firms when business is finished, as they 'file' for it, specifically when they are in difficulties. It is not to say that we have any difficulty yet, it is just that this stage of writing takes us pretty much up to a finish of present business, or more correctly up to date in Real Time as aligned to our actual existence. It is about as far as I my diary page notes go up to. It is where we are now, well through summer in 2005.

As to the future, the way it is, we are no better equipped than anyone else to predict most events, i.e. the future, and therefore can only do a more usual speculation. But it is still forward to the future, that is to say our continued future in witnessing the past, where we can only look to being successful within discovered limitations. We should also limit excursions sensitively, by safeguard of a three-way agreement, as we've set out to do with renewed efforts here in Banna. I am sure soon enough, dad (Prof) will have sufficient supportive recordings for a series of historical writings stacked up ahead of his needs. By then Lewis and I will have satisfied our most immediate, relatively lay interest, in historical truths. It should then remain for us all to review and fully consider, beyond that, how we can give greater benefit to mankind. One good use I am thinking of discussing with the others, would be in crime solving. Of course this is not prevention per say, but certainly as a total physical witness it should have a deterrent effect on perpetrators. Though getting Acceptance Terms to control its use ready and agreed, may well still clash with the unwanted needs of some authorities as interested parties, and then Crime ultimately comes under whoever is Home Secretary.

Then there is also exploration of contemporary areas of danger, directly dangerous environments like Chernobyl, or in natural history with animals dangerous to a cameraman. A further example would be to observe the Sentenelese tribesmen, who simply kill visitors to their stone-age island life.

We will in all fairness give Lewis the principal say in such matters. In that respect we are fortunate that he has non-military pacifist leanings, for it would be soul destroying for the project to become an involuntary contributor to military/political one-upmanship, and maybe at that it would be too dangerous anyway. Though in another respects, not formally revealing excludes Lewis from the recognition he deserves. He should certainly qualify for a Nobel prize, having such a lead in overcoming the time dimension – probably Science and Technology's Man of the Century, but knowing Lewis he'd rather be Man of the Moment, where he'd see a definition of 'moment' as an undefined period of time. Then I harked back to some wise words from my father, when Lewis related to him how he was almost bursting to show and tell, by the time he met and later felt secure with me: "Recognition isn't everything, for there are times when openness is not the way to maximise the impact or usefulness of something and, whilst that stands in the way of recognition, if it is something linked to achievement, that in itself has no bounds if you are not concerned with getting the credit."

But then do we know Lewis well enough - does he want fame? I for one though, would not be surprised if he wanted to do something like that done by Tim Berners-Lee (the creator of www.). An Englishman, who in 1991 gave the details away freely to all concerned at once, of his now commonly used HyperText and Locator programming. In that way he was deliberately giving no one interested party an edge. He did not patent or copyright anything and therefore had no personal commercial gain from it. But in 2004, as it was reported, he became the first person to be awarded the newly established Millennium Technology Prize of $1.2m given for 'outstanding technological achievements that raise the quality of life'. I am sure most would readily agree to that being particularly true. I am then also sure that this sort of label could apply to Lewis.

So, right now if you were in our shoes, what would you do? Accepting the longer-term dilemma, i.e. to expose or not and who to, in this short term where would you want to explore? What would be your choice of historical events, if you had this wonderful opportunity to make retrospective recordings?

In spite of some uncertainty of outcome, I am actually more settled in my general outlook on life, and the way now I see that I can relate to the rest of the world. Not surprisingly, I do see myself as being in an unexpected privileged position, and funnily enough, I always used to motivate myself by thinking that some day I would be 'a man of science' one of the greats. But then we can't all be the principal inventors or discoverers - most do work which are smaller contributions to the whole. Also, as much as I was promoting science and technology background as an essential quality for leadership this century, I've realised that there is another side to the coin, for this at an extreme can be a problem. To blinker knowledge in the opposite way, the blind pursuit of goals has to be reigned in by social responsibility, for example the world at large right now has ethical issues over human genetics.

I've mainly gone along with Lewis' projected ethical aims, with some added useful observations from dad, and as I've suggested, there is nothing wrong with 'playing second fiddle', or less, in just playing a part in such potentially legendary work. I remind myself further of when I was very young and wanted to be one of Santa's helpers. I never thought of being Santa as he pre-existed in the role. So I see now that I need to be happy enough to settle for a mention, or better still to be seen as being on the team, and that of course now includes my father. Possibly a no more firm or lasting bond than to have a relationship go into history. For paired names in an association with achievement, as an example local to our hometown, there was George and Robert Stephenson. Now George deservedly got his image on a banknote, with reference to one of my earlier stated gripes. We'll just have to get Lewis into his best pose, should that happen to him one day, and with my mum's artist skills she could no doubt do a portrait for the purpose, and that at least would mean direct involvement for all four of us. Assuming that is, we haven't had to involve mum anyway, well before such exposure came about, for maybe we would need her expertise in aspects of historical art. I think I can sense, without them actually saying so, that the others feel as I do and would be more comfortable with this becoming a team of four, even though a balanced number can get you into voting deadlock. We may have no choice with this, and more critical aspects of our future and consequent decisions, but to see how it 'pans out' - to use a somewhat pertinent pioneering prospectors' term.

At the close of this broadly satisfactory Friday, I was happy to close my story, and then as 'fate would have it', a term my mother would be pleased that I used, something totally unanticipated happened.

# CHAPTER TWELVE:
## 'THE FLY IN THE OINTMENT'

Next morning I rose lazily, and I knew Dad had said he was going to have an easy morning and treat himself to a six item fried breakfast. When I say 'said', this was more like confiding, as I know mum pushes him more towards grilling if he insists on a Full English (or should we say Irish now that we are here?) This was conveniently after he'd taken mum into Tralee to do some Saturday shopping, and with her not being too familiar with parking opportunities, they agreed best if he delivered and later collected her. By this time, I met with my dad in the corridor, after ascertaining that Lewis was not in his room. "Quick Paul," he said, "let's get some more use of the frying pan for you, and get it straight out of the way well in good time to get the smells away and out of suspicion." Then after we had cooked and ate ours, he did an extra few pieces, saying that he thought Lewis would like a sandwich. That I could take it to him in the outhouse, for he knew Lewis was up early, as they had shared a pot of tea three ways, happily leaving me in my 'pit'.

I did as dad asked, while he washed away the evidence of our 'pigging-out' session. It was a still sunny day, and as I made my way across the ground, I met Lewis just about to come out and head towards me. "Ah, thanks," he said as he took the offering on-a-plate (which it was), "I was just on my way to get you guys. Quick go back for Prof, and I'll get this delight out of the way right here and now meanwhile."

I conveyed the urgency in his voice to dad, who dutifully responded, and we were straight there. Lewis spoke out before we entered, "We've got a 'Fly in the Ointment,' folks!"

As we entered I could not see anything at first, then at our seating-end of the bench, furthest away, I could see a small fuzzy object about the size of a tennis ball. "We've had what you might call a hitchhiker or stowaway," said Lewis as we got closer. "Really!" I puzzled aloud, thinking of animate (biological creatures) and what we'd covered as impossible, followed by the question on all lips, "What is it?" "It was inside, and I think it could well be someone else's probe," said Lewis. I spoke my thoughts and said, "I thought you might say 'alien'." "Certainly 'out of this world' in that it is quite futuristic, and that's what I think we're looking at – some future attempt," said Lewis as he rounded off his accumulated thoughts. This device was about the size of a tennis ball and while we watched it, it changed shape, from a fuzzy sphere, to a tetrahedron, to a cube, then to a sort of three-dimensional, five-pointed star, all within the fuzzy sphere. Then to a solid sphere, via a momentary familiar interstitial shape – that of Lewis' device. All six of these phases just kept repeating, and then we sussed that the 'fuzz only' phase was in fact a line, it then moved through to the opposite geometry of a sphere. "I would suggest we don't touch it," said dad, "how did it get on the bench Lewis?" "I moved it, but naturally I used those old farrier's tongs hanging back up there, I would agree, we don't know what skin contact will do," Lewis replied, "and there's definitely no way into it, it's perfectly sealed to my way of understanding it." "I also think that multi-dimensional changing business is some sort of re-tuning attempt at getting into phase," I said in contribution. "I could understand any attempts to get 'back on track' as it were," said dad, "as it's certainly lost if it's here." "I can only think that it is 3D here, in front of us," said Lewis, "because they have been returned to shape together. But I don't think we've got any choice but to send it back as soon as possible (to 1066) where I think it somehow got onboard, or should I more correctly say inboard, which it could have only done by a space combing process in itself." "So are we clearly saying," I summarised, "that this is also a probe, and is a future example of a time-comb in that it would use the same essential method?" Lewis was nodding in confirmation as I spoke.

Just then there was a loud bang followed by a low rumble which shook the corrugated sides of the building, and we all rushed to the doorway to look out. "I think that was an earth movement, and luckily a bit overdue, from spatial stress because that's here. Having been forcibly returned out of place," Lewis said in quick recognition, "and we can't hang about here, it is to the good that it is nothing like the volume of ours, but we'll still have to act, now! Fortunately I've been re-charging from the moment of return." We scuttled back to the bench, I helped by stowing the cables and I closed up the camera flap fastening it home. Dad quite bravely used the tongs Lewis had referred to, to move and place the 'stranger' inside where Lewis indicated. He in turn was well on with his internal keypad work within the upper panel section, working directly from standing height as before.

We stood back wearing our dark visors as we were used to, but this time we also had a couple of rather dramatic external forking arcs. One of which went through the adjacent roof ventilator panel, and the other across the room and through the open door. "It's ok," affirmed Lewis, "no worries – just stay as you are!" Once we were clear I could not help but go to the doorway which had darkened somewhat, to see whatever I could make of that as a related affect. Sure enough there was a solitary black cloud occupying about a fifth of the clear blue sky, retreating across the fields in the coastal direction, with column of rain underneath it, something which had obviously made its way onward from our dripping wet doorway. This very spectacle I had a chance to relate, after we all walked outside following dad's suggestion to take a breather back at the house.

Making a pot of coffee, dad put the radio on seeking out any news item, and sure enough an announcement came of a measured earthquake with an epicentre around the Dingle Peninsula, low on the Richter scale, but still newsworthy for the British Isles. "Well there we are lad's," he said, an expression which could have accompanied the placing of coffee mugs, or as we knew, some recognition of the fact that we'd actually caused the news.

"What do we say about that experience then," he said as he looked around from side to side at us both hoping for some wisdom, and seeing our simply puzzled and raised eyebrow silent communication, started it rolling with, "I was just thinking of your mum's concerns over unknown traffic this morning, and it now has me thinking – have we got 'unknown traffic' now?" "I thought I'd provided in design for most things allowed as eventualities," said Lewis, "but I didn't 'expect the unexpected' as they say. In a way Paul, it has given you the glimpse into the future, which I know was a route I wouldn't go down in our early discussions." "Funnily enough," I replied, "the prospect of someone probing from our future is something I touched on with dad in our first discussion – the thought that there could be one here looking at us, in principle." " That leads me to say," reflected dad, "just how many are there though? Are they as common as mobile phones are to us – where it has 'grown like topsy' out of nowhere, and are they all hobbyists – are these things even children's toys?" "Yes, we can't know what to predict," I said. "I remember the classic case of IBM and their belief that one per desk and home computing as individual processors, would not be the way of the world, so much so that they just paid to use a ready made operating system (MSDOS) – the rest is history for Microsoft." "I think it stands to reason now that there must be a lot," replied Lewis, "the very fact of our encounter and the probability of that one being able to comb our interspace around itself, means it had to be very close in proximity, though I don't know what that would be, and as an encounter it would have to be a low individual chance." "It may also be that the Battle of Hastings is a popular venue," I suggested, "and fairly precise on time and place, adding to the likelihood of an encounter." There were nods all around as this new problem came into closer focus with us all.

"I would think they might have some system that stops them 'mixing it' like this - wrapping around each other. For if they are freely in use, that is an aspect of harm that they can do," rounded Lewis. "In our case it's a bit like 'Jonah and the Whale'," I remarked, "and there you are dad, I've got memories of you reading me that story." "Certainly true of comparative size," said Lewis. "Yes! Just how will it 'disembark' as it were?" Dad asked. "A very sound question", replied Lewis, "and all I was thinking when I prompted us to act as quickly as we did, was that it needed to be a bit like a getting a 'wasp out of a window', when it obviously came in that way – you can only hope as a matter of course, given sufficient time, that it will go out of it's own accord. There will also, I expect, be some guidance by an owner's system of retrieval at its appointed time." "That's maybe fortunately over and above the case of the wasp," I suggested, "which is often a random, rather than determined event." "Then how far are they coming from in staggered time through the future?" Lewis said as he reasoned things out, "They may have to avoid a lot of traffic as far as they see it, I'll have to think about this some more before we go again, and of course we need ours back here clean."

When we had enough time to explore our initial concerns etc, we then had time, and all had the inclination to continue with a bit more free or 'blue sky' thinking, for we all felt comfortable with each other in expressions without reserve by now. I started, following a sigh with, "Just what was that about? By that I mean what can we believe was behind it?" "I take it you're meaning our future observers. In which case, I can accept that we had a chance encounter," replied dad, "but it has to also mean that Lewis' method has been shown some time in the future, if as Lewis says, they do have a similar technique. It can only mean this or that it was separately discovered later and then used." "Yes, I know just what you're saying," confirmed Lewis, "there's the question, did I satisfy my need now to incorporate some protection, and is this what they then use, which does not give them this 'collision' concern?" "If you're wondering whether this experience played a part in their future, you could be playing on a time paradox," I cautioned, "we just have to say that knowing this did spur you on, then this possible outcome remains in the balance."

Dad thought he would add some future historian's perspective into the consideration, by saying, "We'll have to expect that it is not your lab report that is your last one, and future historians aren't looking into the relevance of 1066 in your path of discovery to give your work some late recognition." "Hey! Maybe it recorded us here," I suggested. "I don't believe so," replied Lewis, "not with the episode we've just witnessed, their device seemed to be in some sort of program loop, seeking or 'tuning' as you said Paul."

"Well, let's make for the preferred future," I said with a new found growing feeling of confidence, which I also believed would become infectious, "I am sure that a proximity detecting solution is within Lewis' capabilities, and I will help in any way I can. You know Lewis that I am more use to you now on logic circuitry and programming then when we first met, thanks to our course and thanks to your untold help with my understanding of the course's electronics lab work." Dad then said he was pleased to hold things until we were happy to proceed, saying in a light but meaningful way, that he would put his back into helping mum on with her horticultural project, in the intended Walled Garden, with a bit more of his labour to earn a crust instead of his writing for now. Lewis was refreshed by both of our standpoints, that he wasn't evidently disappointing dad, and having no doubt heard my declaration of devotion.

The feeling was that there was no time like the present, and so we got a start that day, to work on our contribution to their future in examining the past. This in turn should be telling us that we likely did expose the discovery of Lewis' 'Spatial Combing of the Time Dimension'. It also makes it likely that we'll know when the 'time is right' to do so, and ideally get some say in policy or even licensing for use. Of course right now we've got no way of knowing when or how this may come about, and so we can only see ourselves working on with necessary seclusion here today.